Tennessee
Writers

Tennessee Writers

BY THOMAS DANIEL YOUNG

PUBLISHED IN COOPERATION WITH

The Tennessee Historical Commission

THE UNIVERSITY OF TENNESSEE PRESS

KNOXVILLE

★ TENNESSEE THREE STAR BOOKS/*Paul H. Bergeron, General Editor*

This series of general-interest books about significant Tennessee topics is sponsored jointly by the Tennessee Historical Commission and the University of Tennessee Press. Inquiries about manuscripts should be addressed to Professor Bergeron, History Department, University of Tennessee, Knoxville. Orders and questions concerning titles in the series should be addressed to the University of Tennessee Press, Knoxville, 37916.

Clothbound editions of University of Tennessee Press books are printed on paper designed for an effective life of at least 300 years, and binding materials are chosen for strength and durability.

Library of Congress Cataloging in Publication Data
Young, Thomas Daniel, 1919–
   Literary movements in Tennessee.

   (Tennessee three star books)
   Bibliography: p.
   Includes index.
   1. American literature — Tennessee — History and criticism. 2. Criticism — Tennessee — History.
   3. Tennessee — Intellectual life. I. Title. II. Series.
   PS266.T2Y6   810'.9'9768   81-2206
   ISBN 0-87049-319-1
   ISBN 0-87049-320-5 (pbk.)

ABOUT THE AUTHOR:

Thomas Daniel Young is the Gertrude Conaway Vanderbilt Professor of English at Vanderbilt University. Among his many books are *Gentleman in a Dustcoat: A Biography of John Crowe Ransom,* which won the Jules Landry Award in 1976, and, with M. Thomas Inge, *Donald Davidson: An Essay and a Bibliography.*

Cover Photograph: "The Road to Signal Point," a pastel by Emma Bell Miles, reproduced by permission of Kay and Joe Gaston.

For Alice and Alton

Preface

Certain literary figures who gathered in Tennessee during the first half of this century significantly affected the course of modern American literature. Because three of the most influential movements of twentieth-century literature occurred in Tennessee, I will concentrate on the contributions of those writers who appear now to belong to the true profession of letters.

My intention is to discuss the Fugitives, the Agrarians, and the Southern New Critics as well as the earlier movements of the Southwest Humorists (George Washington Harris) and Local Color (Mary N. Murfree). In addition I will recall the creations of a few contemporaries — particularly those of Taylor, Jones, Agee, and McCarthy. A rather detailed discussion of the novels of Cormac McCarthy is included. He is the youngest member of a group of writers whose work is of very high quality; the tone and thematic concerns of his novels such as *Outer Dark* (1968) and *Child of God* (1973) may be a preview of what to expect from the generation of writers to follow McCarthy. By all of this, I hope to entice the reader to peruse some of our best.

My greatest concern is that I have not been able to provide detailed discussions of many Tennessee writers who deserve more attention than I was able to give within the space limitations of the Three Star Books. Among the writers whom I wish I could have recognized are Rowena Rutherford Farrar, Maristan Chapman, Anne Gordon Winslow, Alfred Leland Crabb, Robert Drake, Robert Rylee, Frances Hodgson Burnett, Frances Boyd Calhoun, Christine Noble Govan, May Justus, William O. Steele, Brainard Cheney, Jesse Wills, Ridley Wills, Merrill Moore, Stanley Johnson, John Trotwood Moore, Stanley Horn, Sidney Mttron Hirsch, and David Morton.

I must express my appreciation to some of the people who have assisted me in the preparation of this book. I am grateful, first of all, to Marice Wolfe, Special Collections Librarian of the Vanderbilt University Library, for allowing me to use photographs from the Jesse E. Wills Collection, to the staff of the Tennessee State Library and Archives for permission to quote from the Ellene Ransom papers, and to Susan Wright, whose knowledge of the complicated process of photographic reproduction is even greater than my ignorance. A list of illustrations, acknowledging their sources, appears elsewhere in the manuscript. John Hindle, Larry Stein, Kyle Young, and Frederick Hull were of invaluable help in assisting with basic research, in offering suggestions, and in proofreading the manuscript. Alberta Martin and Louise Durham typed the several different drafts it passed through in reaching its present stage.

The passage from *A Death in the Family* by James Agee. Copyright © 1938, 1956, 1957, by the James Agee Trust. Reprinted by permission of Grosset and Dunlap, Inc.

Most of all I owe a tremendous debt to my wife, Arlease Lewis Young, without whose assistance and encouragement this book could not have been written.

Nashville, Tennessee   THOMAS DANIEL YOUNG
September 1, 1980

Contents

ILLUSTRATIONS

Tennessee
Writers

1. The South: Old and New

The devastation of the South at the end of the Civil War is well known today by most Americans. There was no money, limited credit, and a serious shortage of ablebodied men needed to re-establish a healthy economy. Added to the natural circumstance were others almost as disastrous: reconstruction policies supported and enforced by vindictive and often unscrupulous men. For example, on March 2, 1867, many of the southern states (but not Tennessee) were placed under military rule, and slightly more than a month later a law was passed in the Congress of the United States requiring all southern men to swear that they had not voluntarily participated in the "rebellion against the United States." The creation of imaginative literature was not given a high priority—the intellectual climate in which, as Sidney Lanier of Georgia proclaimed, "pretty much the whole of life has been in not dying."

Between 1870 and 1900, however, two conflicting ideological groups offered solutions to the problems of the region. The first group, which included Walter Hines Page, Henry W. Grady, and others, are now sometimes referred to as the "Apostles of the New South." The ideas on which these men were in general agreement encompassed the following: (1) with the Civil War over, past sectional disagreements and past sectional agreements should be forgotten; (2) since the plantation system proved impractical, the plantations should be divided, and subsistence farming should be undertaken immediately; (3) the South should industrialize as soon as possible in order to get the capital necessary to insure the success of such a drastic transformation, and leaders in the South should initiate and actively support a program to encourage northern capitalists to invest in southern enterprises.

This generally progressive attitude was opposed by a group of writers who insisted that more than a war had been lost in 1865. A way of life had been destroyed. They thought the experiences of a new age could be expressed without sacrificing the principle on which the older culture was based. Some members of this group, like John Esten Cooke of Virginia, wrote novels idealizing life in the antebellum South. To a large extent, too, Thomas Nelson Page followed Cooke's example and retreated to what he called "the sweetest, purest, most beautiful civilization" the world has ever known, that of the pre-Civil War South. The members of the "New South" group were too materialistic; they were trying, he insisted, to convert his beloved section into a money-worshipping domain. The apostles of the New South were concentrating almost exclusively on what John Crowe Ransom would later call the "economic" forms and neglecting the "aesthetic" forms. Conservative opponents of the New South insisted that the problems of a civilized people respond best to possible solutions based on ethical principles and personal relationships.

The best poet of the South between 1865 and 1920 was Sidney Lanier, who attempted to combine in his poems some of the ideas and attitudes of both of these groups. As did other writers of the section of his time, he had to produce material acceptable to northern publishers (all the publishing firms were located there) and appealing to northern readers. The two most important writers in Tennessee at that time attempted to solve the problems confronting southern writers in different ways. George Washington Harris wrote old Southwest humor, a literary genre very popular throughout the country in the decade before the Civil War. Although the time in which his stories are set is vague, the situations they relate are those that concerned the Old South when parts of the section moved from frontier to civilization. Like George Washington Cable, Sherwood Bonner, and Joel Chandler Harris, Mary Noailles Murfree de-emphasized the controversial social, political, and economic issues that tended to broaden the division between the sections and to exploit the rich tradition of her region. Like her counterparts in other states, she concentrated on idiosyncratic behavior, idiomatic speech, and superstitions and illogical beliefs to demonstrate that the people of the Tennessee mountains were unlike those who had ever existed anywhere else at any other time. The unarticulated motive behind the local color movement seems to have been somewhat as follows: thanks to the Confederacy's surrender at Appomattox we shall soon be one people again; and before the standardization becomes final we should capture the unique characteristics of this strange and exciting section of the country. By reverting to a non-political movement of the Old South, George Washington Harris successfully avoided the divisive sectional strife of his day. Mary Noailles Murfree accomplished the same objective by carefully avoiding controversial social, political, and economic issues while she appeared to emphasize the new spirit of national unity that was sweeping the country.

Between 1830 and 1860 the area from Georgia to Texas — then referred to as the Southwest but for years labeled the Deep South and more recently "the Sun Belt" — underwent rapid transformation. During this period much of the region moved from frontier to civilized society. In this ever-changing social and political situation there appeared a group of lawyers, politicians, teachers, riverboat captains, and representatives of almost all the other professions except the ministry, who undertook to write down the stories they heard around the campfires, on the porches of crossroad stores, or on the barges floating down the river. Although most of these writers were amateurs and published most of their tales either anonymously or pseudonymously, they were among the first writers to render faithfully the dialect of the region. In this respect they look forward to Mark Twain and the local colorists.

Not only did these non-professionals transcribe accurately the speech of the area, they also provided ample examples of its vivid and evocative metaphorical flavor. Simon Suggs, the protagonist of Johnson J. Hooper's *Some Adventures of Captain Simon Suggs,* delineates exactly his parasitic and bloodsucking character when he announces: "Let who will run, gentlemen, Simon Suggs will allers be found stickin thar like a tick onder a cow's belly." He remarks on the fact that ministers always seen to be more attentive to the most attractive young ladies: "Well, who blames 'em? Nater will be nater, all the world over; and I judge ef I was a preacher, I should save the prettiest souls first myself." (In 1856, Hooper, an Alabama newspaperman, who would become secretary of the Confederate senate, published his masterpiece, which in many respects aided in defining the literary genre "Old Southwest Humor.")

That George Washington Harris's protagonist, Sut Lovingood, who proclaims his ineptness at the use of vivid and picturesque language, is being ironic is obvious to anyone who has read the *Sut Lovingood Yarns.* "Now why the devil can't I 'splain myself like yu?" he asks George, a character in most of the stories who speaks conventional English; "I ladles out my words at random, like a calf kickin at yaller-jackids; yu jis' rolls em out tu the pint, like a feller a-laying bricks — every one fits." His description of Mrs. Yardley, a character in one of the stories, is almost as effective: "She looked like she mout been made at fust 'bout four foot long, an' the common thickness ove wimen when they's at tharsefs, an' then had her har tied tu a stump, a par ove steers hitched to her heels, an' then straiched out a-mos' two foot more—mos' ove the straichin cumin outen her laigs an' naik. Her stockins, a-hanging on the clothes-line tu dry, looked like a par ove sabre scabbards, an' her naik looked like a dry beef shank smoked, an' mout been ni ontu es tough." When Parson Bullen, in "Parson John Bullen's Lizards" feels Sut's lizards crawling up his legs, "Old Bullen's eyes wer a-stickin out like ontu two buckeyes flung agin a mud wall, an' he wer a-cuttin up more shines nor a cockroach in a hot skillet."

Anyone who has read many of the yarns of the Old Southwest Humorists realizes that they neither conform to the concept of the Protestant work ethic nor to the restrictions of Victorian morals. They are earthy and robust—and often ribald, bawdy, and sexually suggestive—tales of a people seeking release from a life that is physically demanding and often filled with pain and danger. Above all, they are funny. In many of the stories, activities usually considered as sinful in a society definitely affected by evangelical Calvinism are presented for comic effect. Simon Suggs says that a man "must be shifty to git along in a new country"; therefore he feels no remorse, and the reader is expected to feel none, when Simon steals the collection plate at the camp meeting. (Surely a source for the hilarious camp meeting scene in *Huckleberry Finn.*) Instead of wasting our sympathy on the Reverend Bela Bugg, we are supposed to laugh with Simon because the old rascal has been outwitted and defeated at his own confidence game. Sut Lovingood says his "conshuns felt clar es a mountain spring" even though an involved and very humorous practical joke of his has resulted in the death of two persons.

The tales, particularly those of George Washington Harris, including those of that "Nat'ral Born Durn'd Fool, Sut Lovingood," are often more suggestive of sexual activity than any of the other writing of the time. "One holesum quiltin am wuf three old pray'r meetins on the poperlashun pint," Sut says, "purtickerly ef hits hilt in the dark ove the moon, an' runs intu the night a few hours." On another occasion he tells George that he thinks "quiltins managed in a morrill an' sensibil way, truly am good things—good fur free drinkin, good fur free eatin, good fur free huggin, good fur free dancin, good fur free fitin, an' goodest ove all fur poperlatin a country fas'." "Rare Ripe Garden-Seed" centers around the attempts of a young bride and her mother to convince a husband that the child born four and a half months after his marriage is the result of "a lot ove *rar ripe garden-seed*" bought from a Yankee peddler. The seed speeds all the processes of nature; beans ordinarily mature in three months, but these seeds will produce fully grown beans in six weeks. On one occasion Sut is attempting to explain to George his preference for "widder wimmen": "Hits widders, by golly, what am the rale sensibil, steady-goin, never-skeerin, never-kickin, willin, sperrited, smoof pacers. They cum clost up to the hoss-block, standin still wif thar purty silky years playin, an' the naik-veins a-throbbin, an' waits fur the word, which ove course yu gives, arter yu finds yer feet well in the stirrup, an' away they moves like a cradil on cushioned rockers, ur a spring buggy runnin in damp san'." This passage was written at about the same time Mrs. Nathaniel Hawthorne was going through her husband's private notebooks and blotting out with India ink such words as "bosom," "belch," and "belly." From her industrious pen nothing but a table or a chair escaped with a leg.

Although George Washington Harris was born in Pennsylvania, he grew up in Knoxville, Tennessee, between the Cumberland Plateau and Great Smoky Mountains, the region in which most of his stories are set. Because this section of the country was isolated and sparsely populated, it was largely untouched by the wave of industrialization and urbanization that began to move into the South after the Civil War. Although Harris had less than eighteen months of formal education — because of his manual dexterity he was early apprenticed by his half-brother to work in his jewelry shop — he was a good listener and his sharp ear recorded with fidelity and precision the idioms and rhythms of the regional dialect he heard used every day. No doubt, too, he participated in the camp meetings, quilting parties, wedding celebrations, and all-day singings that gave him the subject matter for some of his satiric, hilariously funny tales of man's predilection for devilment. Although Harris's principal character Sut Lovingood always emphasized his impiety, his love of a practical joke, and his insatiable appetite for "pop-skull whiskey, wimmen, and old sledge," Sut's tales are more than mere fabliaux. The victims of his pranks are usually drunkards, cowards, adulterers, bigots, and hypocrites. The texture of the stories, too, often suggests that their purpose is not mere entertainment.

In the 1840s Harris contributed a few sketches or sporting stories to William T. Porter's *Spirit of the Times,* a New York humor magazine published from 1831 to 1856, in which many of the Old Southwest Humor yarns first appeared. The only Sut story that Harris contributed to this journal was "Sut Lovingood's Daddy, Acting Horse" (1854). Harris's other Lovingood yarns appeared in a variety of newspapers, including the *Knoxville Argus and Commercial Herald,* published by Elbridge G.

Eastman, a friend of his. The only collection of Harris's work to appear in his lifetime was *Sut Lovingood, Yarns Spun by a Nat'ral Born Durn'd Fool* (New York: Dick and Fitzgerald, 1867). During the remainder of the nineteenth century his writings were largely unread, but in this century his admirers, including William Faulkner, have placed him among the very best of the Southwest Humorists. As early as 1930 Franklin J. Meine, one of the first critics to comment extensively on the literary importance of Southwest Humor, was pointing to Harris's "vivid imagination" and declaring that for "sheer *fun,* the *Sut Lovingood Yarns* surpass anything else in American humor." Other scholars have agreed: Walter Blair, another pioneer in the field of American humor, proclaimed that "In *Sut Lovingood,* the antebellum humor of the South reaches its highest level of achievement before Mark Twain." F.O. Matthiessen, one of the most respected critics of the twentieth century, wrote that Harris "brings us closer than any other writer to the indigenous and undiluted resources of the American language." Donald Davidson even traced Sut's speech back to its origin in Devonshire and Southwest England.

Every reader of Harris's stories is impressed with Sut's effective and evocative use of figurative language. Milton Rickels, who has written a book-length study of Harris's humor, has given a good description of this aspect of Harris's art:

> The first effect of [his] frequency of imagery is speed and intensity. The reader is whirled into illusions of sheer delight in motion and wild action. Racy colloquialism, nonce words, corruptions of names and bookish terms, compression of detail, astonishing expansion of connotation, and controlled changes in the tensions of the action and . . . the language, shifting from litotes to the highest hyperbole, give a constant illusion of speed and movement. Images are expanded by piling detail upon detail until the reader is bewildered in a complexity of emotions and ideas.

A rather detailed look at one of Harris's Sut yarns, "Parson John Bullen's Lizards," will demonstrate the texture Rickels is describing. Matthiessen has called this texture a "wonderful kinetic quality" to be found to a comparable degree only in the work of William Faulkner. Along with this distinctive trait are those other characteristics of Harris's artistic genius which motivated M. Thomas Inge in his introduction to *High Times and Hard Times,* a collection of Harris's heretofore uncollected sketches, to proclaim him "the most gifted and original" of the humorists of the Old Southwest and "his creation, Sut Lovingood . . . one of the most genuine, robust, comic figures in American literature."

George sees signs nailed to every tree in the community promising "Ait ($8) Dullars Re-ward" to be paid in "korn, ur urther projuce," to "eny wun what ketches him, fur the karkus ove a sartin wun SUT LOVINGOOD." He takes down one of the posters and sets out in search of Sut to see if he can find out what terrible crime his incorrigible friend has committed. A few days later, he finds Sut, reads the notice to him, and asks for an explanation. "Yas, George, that ar dockymint am in dead yearnist," Sut replies and proceeds to tell him why: "Parson John Bullin" and some of his "hard shells" do want him "the wus kine." Last year at the big meeting at Rattlesnake Springs, Sut continues, he and a friend of his "wer a settin in a nice shady place convarsin." They were sitting in a "huckil berry thickit" doing no harm to anyone, not even making much noise, when "the fust thing I remembers, I woke up from a trance what I hed been knocked inter by a four-year old hickory-stick, hilt in the paw ove ole Passun Bullin." He awoke, Sut says, and Parson Bullen was standing over him, calling him a sinner "an mensunin the name ove my frien' loud enuf tu be hearn tu the meetin 'ous." That night, Sut continues, the parson tells his friend's family what he has seen, and the young lady gets an "all-fired, overhandid stroppin frum her mam." Sut awaits his time to get revenge on that "durnd infunel, hiperkritikal, pot-bellied, scaley-hided, whisky-wastin, stinkin ole groun'-hog."

At the next meeting Sut promises to be converted and takes a seat on the side steps of the pulpit. The weather is fine and the crowd is large and responsive as they sing the opening hymn: "Thar will be mournin, mournin yere, an' mournin thar / On that dredful day tu cum." Then Parson Bullen takes his text: "pow'fly mixed wif brimstone, an' trim'd wif blue flames." He talks to the sinners, "tried tu skeer 'em wif all the wust varmints he oue seen," and after a little while he begins to talk of "Hell-sarpints." He tells them "how the old Hell-sarpints wud sarve em if they didn't repent; how cold they'd crawl over thar nakid bodys, and how like ontu pitch they'd stick tu 'em as they crawled. . . . This were the way they wer tu sarve men folks." Then the parson addressed the women: "tole 'em how they'd quile into thar buzzims, and how they *wud* crawl down onder thar frock strings . . . how sum ove the oldes' an' wus ones wud crawl up thar laigs, an' travil *onder* thar garters, no odds how tight they tied *them,* an' when the two armys ove Hell-sarpents met, then—." This last remark arouses the crowd, Sut says, and of all "the screamin' an' hollerin, and loud cryin, I ever hearn, begun all at onst." Although the hollering and screaming continues, Sut says, he cannot listen, "fur I saw that my time fur ackshun hed cum":

Now yu see, George, I'd cotch seven ur eight big pot-bellied lizzards, an' hed 'em in a littil narrer bag, what I had made a-purpus. Thar tails all at the bottim, an' so crowdid fur room that they cudent turn roun'. So when he wer a-ravin ontu his tip-toes, an' a-poundin the pulpit wif his fis'—onbenowenst tu enybody, I ontied my bag ove reptiles, put the mouf ove hit onder the bottim ove his britches-laig, an' sot into pinchin thar tails. Quick es gunpowder they all tuck up his bar laig, makin a nise like squirrils a-climbin a shell-bark hickory. He stop't preachin rite in the middil ove the word 'damnation,' an' looked fur a moment like he wer a listenin fur sumthin—sorter like a ole sow dus, when she hears yu a whistlin fur the dorgs. The tarifick shape ove his feeters stopp't the shoutin an' screamin; instuntly yu cud hearn a cricket chirp.

In order not to attract attention to himself, Sut begins to moan, as if he is moved by the emotional appeal of the sermon, and places his hands over his eyes and his head between his legs. About this time Parson Bullen goes into action: "He gin hisself sum orful open-handed slaps wif fust one han' an' then tuther, about the place whar yu cut the bes' steak outen a beef. Then he'd fetch a vigrus ruff rub whar a hosses tail sprouts." Then he stamped one foot and then the other. About this time one of the lizzards showed his head above the parson's shirt collar, and he yells: "Pray fur me brethren an' sisteren, fur I is a-rastlin" with the "Hell-sarpints" right now. Suddenly he begins to undress. He jerks off his "clawhammer" coat and flung it behind him like he was going into a fight. He pulls his shirt over his head and jerks his trousers off and takes them by the bottom of the legs and swings them round his head a time or two and flings them on the floor. Out of the pockets come "ni ontu fifteen shorten'd biskits, a boiled chicken wif his legs crossed, a big doubbil-bladed knife, a hunk ove terbaker, a cob-pipe, sum copper ore, lots ove broken glass, a cork, a sprinkil ove whiskey, a squirt, and three lizzards." One of the lizzards went down the "buzzim ove a fat 'oman, es big as a skin'd hoss an' nigh onto es ugly. . . . She were jis' boun' tu faint; an' she did hit fust rate."

By this time the Reverend Mr. Bullen is completely undressed except for his shoes and socks. He yells, "Brethren, brethren, take keer ove yerselves, the Hell-sarpints hes got me" and leaps into the crowd. He lands on "Old Misses Chaneyberry" who "sot wif her back tu the pulpit, sorter stoopin forrid," shutting her up like a jack-knife. Then he runs through the crowd "in a heavy lumberin gallop, like a ole fat waggon hoss, skared at a locomotive." As he runs, he opens "a purfectly clar track to the woods, ove every living thing. He weighed ni ontu three hundred, had a black stripe down his back, like ontu a ole bridil rein, an' his belly were 'bout the size an' color ove a beef paunch, an' hit a-swingin out frum side tu side; he leand back frum hit, like a littil feller a-totin a big drum." He is last seen disappearing in the bushes.

All of this occurred six months ago and "Ole Barbelly Bullin es they calls him now, never preached ontil yesterday, an' he hadn't the fust durn'd 'oman tu hear 'im; *they hev seed too much ove 'im.*" Like all the best of Harris's yarns, this one has an ulterior motive. Although it has lived for its vivid and authentic reproduction of rural southern idiomatic speech and its well-paced delivery of an appropriately exaggerated and hilariously funny story based on actual folk customs, it also exposes physically and spiritually a hypocritical and guileful fraud. Harris's was humor with a purpose.

At the end of the Civil War there was intense concern for and interest in things southern. In 1873, Edward King, on assignment for *Scribner's Monthly,* toured the South with a photographer and gathered material for a series of articles and sketches published serially in *Scribner's* as *The Great South.* In New Orleans, King became acquainted with the work of George Washington Cable and sent two of his stories back to New York; one of these, "'Sieur George," appeared in *Scribner's* in October 1873. The popularity of King's pieces and Cable's story prompted *Harper's Monthly* to assign Edwin DeLeon to do a series called *The New South,* and the southern Local Color movement was underway. Writers in all sections of the South began to exploit the traditions of their region. Cable was joined by Kate Chopin and Grace Elizabeth King in writing stories about the quaint and bizarre customs of the Creoles and Cajuns of New Orleans. Joel Chandler Harris wrote his Uncle Remus stories based on the unique superstitions, attitudes, and behavior patterns of the southern blacks. John Esten Cooke and Thomas Nelson Page produced their novels depicting life on the Virginia plantation. Sherwood Bonner celebrated the life of the hillbillies of Mississippi and the mountaineers of Tennessee. In the latter of these endeavors her work was surpassed in quantity—and perhaps in quality as well—by that of Mary Noailles Murfree.

Mary Murfree grew up on a twelve-hundred-acre plantation, near Murfreesboro, Tennessee, a town named for her family. Her father, himself a lover of books, saw that Mary, her brother, and her sister were amply supplied with reading materials, particularly with the works of the better-known nineteenth-century English novelists. Left slightly lame by a childhood illness, Mary lived a rather secluded life, sharing her literary interests with her brother, sister, and father, who often read aloud to the entire family, and her fondness for music with her mother, an accomplished musician. Mary and her sister Fanny attended the Nashville Female Academy, studied French with a French governess, were taught Latin, mathematics, and Spanish by their father, and completed their formal education by attending for two years the Chegary Institute in Philadelphia.

For fifteen years the entire Murfree family spent their summers at Beersheba Springs, a popular watering place of that time in the Cumberland Mountains. Mary and Fanny also spent some time in the Great Smoky Mountains. In both of these settings Mary was able to observe closely the peculiarities of manners and customs of the natives, as her sharp ear was accurately recording the rhythm and sound of their idiomatic speech. In her youth Mary's father had encouraged her to write some stories, set in Mississippi and Kentucky, employing the Negro, Irish, and mountain dialects spoken by the natives of those regions. Later, after reading some of the local color stories with which the journals of the time were filled — and particularly a story of Rebecca Harding Davis's about the North Carolina mountaineers — she decided to write about the natives whose strange and unusual speech and behavior she had observed at Beersheba Springs. According to Fanny, Mary wanted to preserve the unique speech and behavior patterns of the Tennessee mountaineers — as other writers were doing for other regions — before the railroads, urbanization, and standardization destroyed them forever.

She began, therefore, a novel about these people she had observed so carefully during her summers at Beersheba Springs. After she had completed the first chapter, both she and her sister agreed that it was complete in itself; consequently she decided to try to publish it as a short story. Thinking its chances of being accepted would be enhanced had it been written by a man, she submitted it to William Dean Howells, editor of *The Atlantic Monthly,* under the pseudonym of Charles Egbert Craddock (she had earlier published under the name of R.E. Dembry). Howells accepted the story, and it appeared as "The Dancin' Party at Harrison's Cove" in the *Atlantic* for May 1878. Howells published four other

---

Mary Noailles Murfree at about age thirty. *University of Tennessee Press.*

of the Craddock stories: "The Star in the Valley" (November 1878), "Electioneerin' on Big Injun Mounting" (January 1880), "The Romance of Sunrise Rock" (December 1880), and "Over on T'other Mounting" (June 1881). Howells's successor, Thomas Bailey Aldrich, published three others: "The 'Harnt' that walks Chilhowee" (May 1883), "A-Playin' of Old Sledge at the Settlemint" (October 1883), and "Drifting Down Lost Creek" (March and April 1884). At the urging of Aldrich, the publishers Houghton Mifflin issued all of these stories as *In the Tennessee Mountains* (1884), the best of her ten novels and thirty-five short stories set in the Tennessee mountains of her time. Of the twenty-five books she published, the action of twenty-two of them occurs in her native state, and despite some obvious flaws of plotting and characterization, no one else has produced as much fiction about the people of Tennessee or rendered more accurately the dialect of the region.

The same year that *In the Tennessee Mountains* was published, J.R. Osgood brought out *When the Battle Was Fought,* and the next book, *Down the Ravine,* was serialized by *Wide-Wake,* after which Houghton issued it in book form. Almost simultaneously *The Atlantic Monthly* carried *The Prophet of the Great Smoky Mountains* in seven installments. Again Houghton published this book, hard upon the heels of *Down the Ravine.* The name of no other author was more constantly before the eyes of the American reader in the early 1880s than that of Charles Egbert Craddock. As her stories became more popular, it was increasingly difficult for Miss Murfree to conceal the identity of her pseudonym. In 1884, for example, a St. Louis newspaper, where the Murfrees were then living, carried a brief note: "Another cold potato thrown at history. Charles Egbert Craddock isn't C.E.C. at all, but Mr. M.N. Murfree of St. Louis." From all quarters the family was bombarded with questions about the identity of Mr. M.N. Murfree. It soon became evident that the secret could not be kept much longer. The family discussed the matter at some length and finally concluded, as Fanny Murfree indicated in an unpublished biography of her sister, "it was decided that it would be neither wise nor courteous to allow a disclosure of a kind touching their own affairs to be made to the publishers through some newspaper." Mr. Murfree insisted, therefore, that Mary and Fanny arrange a meeting with Thomas Bailey Aldrich, which they promptly did. Fanny Murfree records Aldrich's astonishment when a slight, crippled spinster walked into the office of *The Atlantic Monthly* and announced she was Charles Egbert Craddock, the author of those action-filled, masculine-dominated stories of the Tennessee mountains. First he announced to his office staff that those ladies were sisters of Charles Egbert Craddock and hurried them into his private office.

> "[T]he next evening came the memorable dinner. The guests were Oliver Wendell Holmes, Lawrence Barrett, and Mrs. James T. Fields. Miss [Sarah Orne] Jewett was ill and Edwin Booth sent regrets, as he never dined out on evenings that he played. W.D. Howells came in, although, having an engagement, he could not stay for dinner. As the guests were successively introduced to 'Mr. Craddock,' whom they had all been invited to meet, their surprise was supreme—most of all that of Mrs. Fields . . . [who] persistently called her 'Miss Craddock.'"

After dinner the party went to the theater, and Aldrich went back stage between acts and identified "Mr. Craddock" to Booth as "the fellow in the front of the box, with the red rose in his bonnet." In this manner was the best kept literary secret of the nineteenth century revealed.

Murfree's art is severely restrained by the literary genre to which it belongs. After the local color writer has rendered faithfully or romantically his setting and recorded the odd behavior, the unusual customs and superstitions of the people of the region, as well as their unique manner of speech, there remains little for him to do. No plausible action that he could invent would be as interesting or compelling as the characteristics he has presented. Local color stories follow, therefore, a predictable pattern. At least the first third of the story is consumed with presenting in elaborate detail the setting and rendering as precisely as possible the strange customs and beliefs, usually based on superstition, and the bizarre behavior of the people. When the basic conflict of the story is introduced, usually a third or a half of the author's space has been used, and the part of the story that should command our closest attention, as we move through a series of resolved or unresolved complications toward a resolution of the conflict, is usually disappointing. Our most profound interest is not in *why* the characters do what they do; they act as they do because they *are* the kind of people they are. The extent to which the story commands our attention depends entirely upon the degree to which we are fascinated by the strange behavior of the characters. The author succeeds only if he convinces us not only that his characters speak a strange idiom but that they act in a manner peculiarly their own.

Miss Murfree's principal claim to fame is succinctly stated by Professor Nathalia Wright in her introduction to *In the Tennessee Mountains,* Murfree's least flawed collection of stories:

It would seem, in fact, that the southern mountaineers do not inspire individualized fictional treatments as do their kinsmen the poor whites — from the Georgia crackers of Longstreet to the Mississippi share-croppers of Faulkner. These mountaineers, like those everywhere — and like most of the characters of all local color fiction — have achieved identity as a social group and in a circumscribed environment. Their culture, like that of all arrested groups, is static, a fact about all such groups which limits their usefulness to fiction. Though Miss Murfree does not make this point about Tennessee mountain culture explicitly, she implies as much throughout her first book about it, in her representation of the mountaineers and the mountains as by nature inseparable. The implication, indeed, may be her most significant achievement.   (xxxiii)

Like Mary Noailles Murfree, Emma Bell Miles (1879–1919) was a local color writer. Born in Indiana, she spent her adolescent years at the foot of Walden's Ridge, an escarpment of the southern Cumberlands terminating near Chattanooga. Although she was a member of a relatively poor family, by late adolescence her artistic accomplishments — then mostly in painting — had brought her the attention and company of the cultured, wealthy elite of Chattanooga, some of whom even sent her to St. Louis to study art. After two years she returned to marry her childhood sweetheart, Frank Miles, a descendant of one of the original mountain families, who had settled on Walden's Ridge before the Civil War. For the remainder of her troubled and unhappy life — her marriage was far from perfect and for many years she was ravaged by disease — she lived in her beloved Appalachian mountains. She died at the age of forty, a victim of tuberculosis.

Although she wrote a little verse and short fiction, her literary reputation today is based on *The Spirit of the Mountains* (1905), her only published novel. Like most of her contemporaries, she employed in her fiction the conventions of the regional writer. Her narrative is related by an outsider, a school teacher who speaks in correct standard English and occasionally comments on the strange behavior and superstitious beliefs of the mountain people. Unlike that of most of her contemporaries, however, Miles's work demonstrates a careful attention to the rhythm and sounds of Appalachian speech and a sincere respect for mountain customs and traditions. "Emma Bell Miles," as one critic points out, "is at her best . . . in discussing the relationship between men and women in the mountains, and the effect of economic change upon mountain culture and society."

In addition to a few poems and regional stories, which appeared in *Century, Harper's, Lippincott's, Putnam's,* and other similar journals, *The Spirit of the Mountains* was her only published work. In her strict attentions to the details of the dialectical speech of her characters, the attempt for authenticity in the presentation of Appalachian manners, beliefs and customs, and her obvious respect for the morals, integrity, and dignity of the mountain people she writes about, Emma Bell Miles's fiction certainly deserves more attention than it is presently receiving.

With the exception of Harris, Murfree, and Miles, not much literature of lasting value was created in Tennessee between 1865 and 1920. The situation in Tennessee was not markedly different, however, from that in the South generally. The most important poets were Sidney Lanier and Paul Hamilton Hayne, and few people today, except literary specialists, know much of either poet's work. In fiction, perhaps because of the demands of northern periodicals for southern materials, the quality of the writing was a little better. Being as generous as one can, however, he is hard pressed to find much of genuine literary merit, with the exceptions noted, coming from Tennessee before the Fugitives began publishing their little magazine in April 1922. David Morton wrote a considerable number of structurally correct but unimpressive sonnets. His literary gift was obviously limited. Grantland Rice, the sports writer, composed at least one poem, a portion of which seems to be repeated by every speaker at any athletic banquet: "He marks—not whether you won or lost—but how you played the game."

A quick perusal of the many volumes of *The Library of Southern Literature* will convince one that most of what appears there can be called literature only under the most liberal definition of poetry and prose fiction. In fact there seems little that appeared after Edgar Allan Poe and William Gilmore Simms to prepare us for the phenomenon that occurred in Nashville during the second decade of this century. Almost by accident, it would appear, a group of young men, many of whom were students and professors at Vanderbilt University, met informally to talk of religion, philosophy, and literature. These conversations ushered in that which we have come to know as the Southern Literary Renaissance. After several years of these more-or-less accidental meetings, the group began to meet informally but on a regular schedule. Shortly, thereafter, they published the first issue of *The Fugitive,* the initial creative act of one of the most influential literary groups in twentieth-century America.

2. The Fugitives

In the summer of 1914 a small group of Vanderbilt students began visiting a Jewish mystic and writer, Sidney Mttron Hirsch, at the apartment of his parents on Twentieth Avenue, just two blocks from the campus. Among those who first attended these informal gatherings were Donald Davidson, Alec B. Stevenson, William Yandell Elliott, and Stanley Johnson, but soon Walter Clyde Curry and John Crowe Ransom joined the group. The discussions at these sessions were usually continuations of subjects introduced in one of the classes at Vanderbilt or of questions raised in the voracious reading programs in which all members of the group were engaged. Elliott wrote Stevenson, who was spending some time in Canada with relatives, that "last night the company was Olympian" and the conversation was "The Happiness": the conversation, he wrote, was a discussion of the "Unity of Being" with Ransom "maintaining a dualism at least—*Elan Vital* and Material Expression, I admitting a logical duality, maintaining a pluralistic Individuality of Being, but a Metaphysical Unity." The quality of the discussion at these meetings is indicated by Donald Davidson in *Southern Writers in the Modern World:* "[The discussions] ranged through poetry to philosophy, but became predominantly philosophical whenever in those years Ransom, Elliott, and Johnson led the conversation into some logical dispute, as it seemed to me they too often did. Like Stephen Dedalus in Joyce's *Portrait of the Artist* I felt myself destined to be but a shy guest at the feast of the world's great culture if the banquet were to consist of the categories of Kant and the heresies of Hegel."

These discussions continued until the group dispersed to serve in the military forces in World War I. When war was declared in Europe in 1914, talk in the Fugitive group naturally turned toward the issues involved in that conflict. Even these discussions were heated because many members of the group disagreed violently in their attempts to fix the degree of guilt that lay with the two antagonists. Before America en-

tered the war, sentiment on the Vanderbilt campus was not predominantly pro-Ally. In 1915, remembering his long summer visits in Germany while he was a Rhodes scholar, Ransom wrote an essay entitled
"The Question of Guilt" and published it in *The Yale Review*. The burden of this piece is that both sides have equally tenable arguments regarding the question of right and wrong—as did the North and South in
the Civil War—and Ransom argues that neither the Central Powers nor
the Allies has an unchallenged claim on justice. The tragedy, he concludes, is that two just and right causes must remain irreconcilable. Too,
Professor H.C. Sanborn of the philosophy department, and one of the
most popular and influential members of the faculty, had received most
of his graduate education in Germany. "He had absorbed the technique
and spirit of German education," Professor Edwin Mims, chairman of
the English department, declared; consequently his cogent pro-German
arguments affected the views of many of his young followers.

After America entered the war, however, any anti-Ally support was
quickly silenced. Vanderbilt Chancellor James H. Kirkland called Professor Sanborn into his office and explained that all members of his faculty were loyal Americans and supported their country in its fight
against Germany and the Central Powers. The campus began to organize its activities as much as possible to support the war effort. In their
classrooms the professors vocally supported the Allied cause, war bond
rallies were held on the campus, and physical education classes were
converted into drill sessions. The Hirsch circle dispersed and most of its
members joined the armed forces. Ransom served as an artillery officer
in France, as did Alec Stevenson. Davidson was a first lieutenant in the
infantry, and William Elliott and Stanley Johnson were attached to
army units fighting in France.

After the Armistice (1918), since the army did not have a sufficient
number of ships to return all of the soldiers to America immediately, it
allowed those qualified and interested to attend special courses offered
by European universities. Ransom enrolled at different times at both the
universities of Grenoble and Nancy, Elliott took courses at the Sor-
bonne, and Stevenson studied at the University of Clermont. Although
Davidson returned home as soon as possible to see his wife, Theresa
Sheresa—whom he had married while he was in the army—and his
daughter, Mary, who was born while he was overseas, he was financially
unable to return immediately to Vanderbilt. As a consequence he spent
the academic year 1919–20 at Kentucky Wesleyan College. Only the
combination of a summer position on the *Nashville Evening Tennessean*

and the offer of a teaching fellowship in the English department at Vanderbilt convinced him that he could undertake a course of study leading toward his master's degree.

By 1921 most of the members were back in Nashville and the discussions continued in a new location, at the home of James M. Frank on Whitland Avenue. New members joined the group—Frank, William Frierson, and Allen Tate—and the nature of the discussions drastically changed, from animated conversations centering on general philosophical questions and the impact of scientific discoveries and the higher criticism of the Bible on man's faith to technical discussions of the craft of writing poetry. The reason for this sudden change is not entirely clear. The most logical explanation seems to be that Ransom had become firmly fixed as the intellectual leader of the group—though Hirsch remained the official host—and he was interested in the *craft* of poetry, an interest he had always demonstrated in his classes and one that had been fed by his introduction to the Symbolist poetry of France. Too, he was now a published poet, his *Poems About God* (1919) having appeared while he was serving in France. There was also the addition to the group of Allen Tate, who brought to each session a commanding knowledge of and an intense and infectious interest in modern theories and practices of art. Primarily as a result of the influence of these two men, the conversations at the sessions became specifically literary, with a decided emphasis on poetic forms. Soon each member, in turn, was asked to bring to a meeting an original poem or poems, with a copy for each member of the group.

In *Southern Writers in the Modern World* Davidson gives an explicit description of these meetings. After the poet had read his poem aloud, he writes, there was usually a "murmur of compliments," often followed by a period of "ruminative silence." When the discussion began, its animation was likely to vary in proportion to the quality of the poem under consideration. The better the poem the more intense the discussion, and it was likely "to be quite ruthless in its exposure of any technical weaknesses as to rhyme, meter, imagery, metaphor and was often minute in

---

Above: The Fugitives in 1956—(back row, left to right) William Y. Elliott, Merrill Moore, Jesse Wills, Sidney Hirsch; (middle row) Alfred Starr, Alec B. Stevenson, Robert Penn Warren; (front row) Allen Tate, John Crowe Ransom, Donald Davidson. *Below:* Donald Davidson, a first lieutenant in the infantry. *Photographs from Jesse E. Wills Collection.*

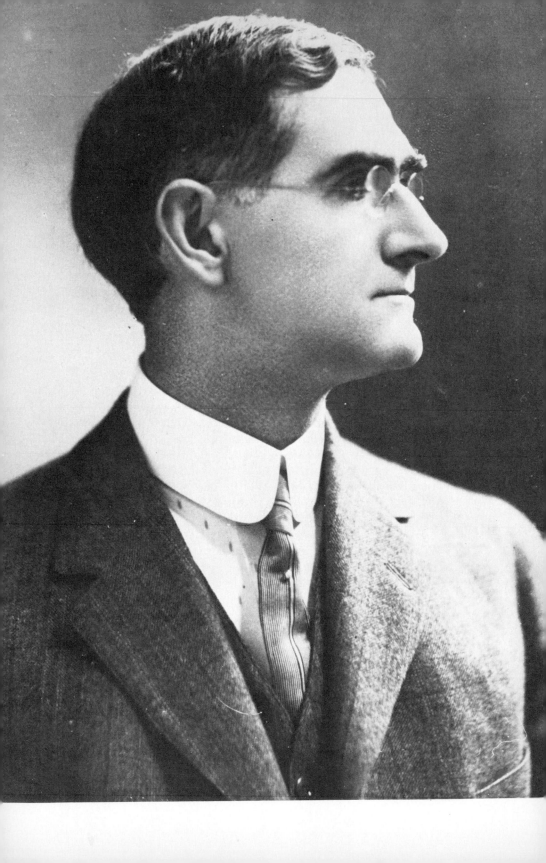

analysis of details." (These were much similar to the discussions that had been occurring in Ransom's classes for a decade.) Since the group included both traditionalists—Hirsch, Johnson, Elliott, and Frank—and modernists—Tate, Ransom, and Davidson—the opinion of a poem's merits might be sharply divided. Unless the poem was of potentially high literary quality, it did not attract much comment. (Such candid and helpful criticism of a young poet's efforts while he was creating his poems apparently has occurred nowhere else in the South.) Often the poet would revise his work in the light of the criticism he had received and bring it back for a second, and sometimes even for a third, reading.

In March 1922 Hirsch suggested that the members of the group had written enough poetry of merit to justify the publication of a small journal, and in April of that year the first issue of *The Fugitive*—the name was suggested by Stevenson—appeared, and, as Professor William Pratt has indicated, in the introduction to his anthology, *The Fugitive Poets,* "the period of modern Southern literature had begun." The journal had no editor so the poems carried in this first issue were selected by vote. The cost of publication was shared equally by each member; most of the proofreading and other editorial work of this kind was done by Davidson. The journal was produced by the least expensive printer the group could find. Although the actual work of addressing the copies for mailing was shared, Davidson answered most of the correspondence the journal received. He performed, therefore, many of the editorial duties associated with the production of such a journal. (This method of operation was later changed and an editor and associate editor were selected for each issue. Finally these officers were elected to serve for an entire year.)

The first issue of the magazine carried poems, under pseudonyms, of only the "seven of friends"—the phrase is Ransom's—Ransom, Davidson, Tate, Stevenson, Johnson, Curry, and Hirsch. In the second issue the seven became nine, including poems by Merrill Moore and James Frank; the third issue (October 1922) published a poem by William Elliott. When the last issue of the journal, the nineteenth, appeared in 1925, the masthead carried the names of fourteen members—Alfred Starr, Robert Penn Warren, Jesse Wills, Ridley Wills, and Laura Riding Gottschalk having been added and William Elliott dropped.

The first issue of *The Fugitive* carried a foreword which announced

---

James M. Frank about 1915. *Jesse E. Wills Collection.*

clearly and straightforwardly the intentions of the new publication: "Official exception having been taken by the sovereign people to the mint julep, a literary phase known rather euphemistically as Southern literature has expired, like any other stream whose source is stopped up. . . . The Fugitive flees from nothing faster than the high-caste Brahmins of the Old South. Without raising the question of whether the blood in the veins of its editors runs red, they at any rate are not advertising it as blue."

In this same issue in his poem "Ego," not one of his best, Ransom indicates a feeling of isolation, a separation from the society out of which he came:

> You have heard something muttered in my scorn:
> "A little learning addleth this man's wit,
> He crieth on our dogmas Counterfeit!
> And no man's bubble 'scapeth his sharp thorn;
>
> "Nor he respecteth duly our tall steeple,
> But in his pride turning from book to book
> Heareth our noise and hardly offereth look,
> Nor liveth neighborly with these the people."

Only his "seven of friends," the poets in this volume, share his feelings, attitudes, and convictions:

> So I take not the vomit where they do,
> Comporting downwards to the general breed;
> I have run further, matching your heart and speed,
> And tracked the Wary Fugitive with you;

When the magazine was discontinued three and a half years later, it had served as a definite force in shaping the careers of one of the most influential and articulate literary groups in twentieth-century America. No other coterie of poets, as Professor Pratt points out, has "shown greater perseverence in directing" the course of modern letters. Only the Imagists, a group of poets who insisted on attempting to produce the natural physical image without endowing it with any emotional or intel-

---

Above: Home of James M. Frank, where the Fugitives met, 1920–1928. *Photograph courtesy of Susan Wright. Below:* Vanderbilt Board of Trust dinner, 1956—(left to right) Allen Tate, Merrill Moore, Mrs. Moore, William Y. Elliott, Mrs. Elliott, Jesse Wills, Mrs. Wills, Robert Penn Warren. *Jesse E. Wills Collection.*

lectual content, have had as much influence on shaping poetic style in America in this century. The four leading literary figures among the Fugitives—John Crowe Ransom, Allen Tate, Donald Davidson, and Robert Penn Warren—were genuine men of letters and, among them, made important contributions to a variety of literary genres: the novel, drama, poetry, short story, and literary criticism. These men were members of three of the most significant literary movements of the present century: the Fugitives, the Agrarians, and the New Critics. (Davidson always denied, however, that he was a New Critic.)

Before *The Fugitive* ceased publication it had published almost all of Ransom's mature verse. In it appeared almost all of those ten or twelve poems, which, Allen Tate said, established him as "one of the greatest elegiac poets in the language." These are the same poems which Randall Jarrell, one of the most perceptive commentators on modern verse, insisted "will always be read and cared for" because they are "perfectly realized and occasionally almost perfect." These are the poems that Isabel Gamble MacCaffrey asserts, in her seminal study of Ransom's poetry, provide "an accurate mirror of the modern sensibility" because they reflect "the miraculous virtues of contemporary verse at its best: its combination of delicacy and strength, of fervor with restraint, of elegance with earthiness." In fewer than a hundred poems, most of them published in *The Fugitive,* Ransom was able to represent with great accuracy and precision the "inexhaustible ambiguities, the paradoxes and tensions, the dichotomies and ironies that make up the life of modern man." It was Ransom's compelling interest in poetry, after the publication of *Poems About God* (1919), that altered the nature of the Fugitives' meetings, and the contents of his other two books of original verse —*Chills and Fever* (1924) and *Two Gentlemen in Bonds* (1927)—were written while that group was holding its regular sessions, meetings as aesthetically stimulating as any held anywhere in America in the twentieth century.

If the poetry of Ransom made *The Fugitive* one of the most important magazines of verse published in modern America, the regular appearance of this journal also aided materially in the development of the literary careers of Allen Tate, Donald Davidson, and Robert Penn Warren. In its pages Tate had the opportunity to test some of his modernistic theories and techniques against the traditional sensibility and the classically trained mind of John Crowe Ransom. The head-on confrontation between these two highly gifted artists helped Tate to find his poetic voice, and to a large extent his poetic vocabulary, so that later in his career he could include Ransom, along with T.S. Eliot, as the two men who were the greatest influences on his literary career. Publication in *The Fugitive* assisted Davidson in finding the kind of poetry he wanted to write — the long, quasi-narrative, philosophical, meditative verse found in such books as *The Tall Men* (1927). Surely Warren profited immensely at the outset of his brilliant and prolific career, as he has admitted on many occasions, from the opportunity to have his early verse read by and commented on by some of the most perceptive and gifted literary critics of the century.

In the December 1925 issue of *The Fugitive* Ransom announced that "with this issue *The Fugitive* suspends regular publication." Since a little later in the statement he revealed that "no financial exigency was the joint in our armour" and that "from the literary standpoint there is no stoppage in the quantity or the quality of Fugitive output," there has been considerable speculation on why the journal was discontinued. Since the financial condition of the magazine was the soundest it had even been, and there was no scarcity of poems of sufficient literary merit to justify publication, the question is: Why did *The Fugitive* cease publication? The first reason, and maybe the most important one, is that no one capable of functioning as editor was willing to devote the time required to serve in that capacity for a magazine attracting international attention, as *The Fugitive* then was. It seems, too, that the four writers who had served as its nucleus no longer felt the urgent need for the journal that they once did. With the publication of his third book of poetry, and with his best poetry behind him, Ransom's interest in writing poetry was less compelling than it had been. Now he was eager to write a critical book on the nature and function of poetry, a subject he had brooded over for ten years or more. The only tangible results of his interest in theoretical criticism were a few brief essays for *The Fugitive* and a review of *The Waste Land* for *The Literary Review* of the *New York Evening Post*. During 1926 and much of 1927, therefore, Ransom spent most of his creative energy composing "a general aesthetic of poetry," a book-length critical manuscript which he later "consigned to the flames" when he became convinced that "such studies can scarcely afford to be pursued in any way except in the constant company of actual poems." Then he turned to writing *The World's Body,* the theoretical basis of much of the formalist criticism written in America since its appearance.

After two or three years of attempting to write, under Allen Tate's tutelage, modernist verse — poems that rearrange, remake, or remold the naturalistic order of things in an attempt to represent accurately the poet's view of reality — Davidson discovered about 1925 the kinds of poems he wanted to write: they were not the brief lyrics — such as "Dryad," "Naiad," and "Corymba" — which he had composed in an attempt to illustrate the theory of correspondences, "that an idea out of one class of experience may be dressed up in the vocabulary of another." Although it is true, that in these poems Davidson finds the subject matter of his later poetry, he turned from the brief experimental verses he had been writing for *The Fugitive* to the largely autobiographical, blank-verse narratives that form *The Tall Men* (1925). As Louise Cowan, the literary historian of the Fugitives, has noted, Davidson had concluded that he could not be a "detached observer of society, isolated from it." He felt that he must be "*with* society not *against* it"; therefore he attempted to write a poem that would blend his personal past with that of his region. The poem is a connected sequence of ten philosophical narratives running to more than a hundred pages in which a modern southerner attempts to examine his heritage. He "journeys" down the "long street" that leads him back into his traditional heritage, beginning with the settlement of Tennessee by the "Tall Men," the early pioneers, and moving through the development of the antebellum South, the catastrophic effects of the Civil War and its disastrous aftermath. After his treatment of the past, he turns toward the present, the southerner's participation in World War I, his marriage to a girl outside the South, and his attempts to form an integrated pattern of the fragmentary chaos of the 1920s. He finally concludes that the present world, one that seems to drift from one position to another without a strongly focused body "of common beliefs," is vastly inferior to the world of "aim and purpose" that had existed before its "common beliefs" were destroyed by religious skepticism, applied science, and modern technology. His conclusion in the last poem in the series, then, is that the aimless, purposeless present can be contrasted at almost every point with the heroism and humanism of a living past.

Just as Davidson's developing literary career led naturally from the kind of verse published in *The Fugitive* to a different type of poetry, Tate's compelling desire to devote his life to a career in letters forced him to seek areas of literary activity much more professional than that which had dominated *The Fugitive*. He felt the need of literary associations not available in Nashville, where poetry, though a serious pursuit by some of the Fugitives, was nevertheless an avocation. Early in June 1924, therefore, even before *The Fugitive* ceased publication, Allen Tate visited his mother in Washington, D.C. and made his way on to New York, determined to make every sacrifice possible in an attempt to earn his living by literary journalism so that he could devote himself completely to the world of letters. In New York, Tate met the most noted members of the New York literati, with some members of which he would form life-long friendships. In June 1924, while visiting Warren in Guthrie, Kentucky, Tate met Caroline Gordon, from nearby Trenton, Kentucky, whom he had never met but whose writing he had admired, particularly an early assessment of the Fugitives which had appeared in a Chattanooga newspaper. She, too, wanted to write professionally, so the two young people found they had much in common. When Tate returned to New York, therefore, he invited Caroline to join him, and on November 2, 1924, the young couple was married. In order to eke out the scantiest livelihood, Tate wrote reviews and brief literary feature essays for the *Nation,* the *New Republic,* and the *New York Herald-Tribune,* and Caroline for the first time devoted most of her time to writing serious fiction. For a time, too, Tate supplemented his meager income by serving as an assistant to the editor of the pulp magazine, *Telling Tales.* At the same time he continued to write verse, publishing in little magazines covering a broad spectrum the first of his poems to command serious attention outside the Fugitive group. He also wrote two biographies — *Stonewall Jackson: The Good Soldier* (1928) and *Jefferson Davis: His Rise and Fall* (1929) — and published his first volume of verse, *Mr. Pope and Other Poems* (1928).

In 1925–26 Tate was deeply engrossed in writing his best-known poem, "Ode to the Confederate Dead," which he continued to revise for the next ten years. Although the poem carries the word "Ode" in its title, it is not an ode — a kind of poem which in the Greek poet Pindar's time was composed to celebrate an important state occasion — and although the poem is written in the loose three-part structure of the genre that was employed as late as the eighteenth century — strophe, antistrophe, and epode — Tate informed Davidson that he really wrote the poem to demonstrate that the form was inaccessible to the modern poet. "Fragmentary chaos" has succeeded the "active faith" of a traditional society, the poem insists, and try as he may, the protagonist of the poem, a modern man sitting late one autumn afternoon at the gate of a Confederate cemetery, cannot imagine that the falling leaves are the "charging soldiers" of the Confederacy who lie buried in the graves before him. He is aware of the changing seasons in "the falling leaves" of autumn; but he has lost the faculty of explaining mystery through myth upon which the members of a traditional society once relied as a means of addressing the mysteries that transcend reason and sensory experience. At the time Tate subscribed to Oswald Spengler's theory that all cultures move through cycles that go from youth, when they possess vitality and purpose, to a final stage of decay leading to destruction and disappearance. Western European civilization, Spengler argued, was going through its final stage; Tate was convinced, therefore, that dynamic art could not be produced in a dying age. On May 14, 1926, he wrote Donald Davidson that he agreed with T.S. Eliot, the expatriate American poet, that "there are no important themes for modern poets. Hence we all write lyrics; we must be subjective."

As Tate was reading and absorbing the intellectual skepticism of Spengler, he was also studying the literary criticism of T.E. Hulme, the early twentieth-century British critic, whose principles gave "philosophic support to modern poetry's predilection for the concrete image, the finite terrain, the employment of wit and above all spiritual and intellectual skepticism." These attitudes and concepts Tate brought to the discussions of the Fugitives — as well as the theories and practices of Eliot and Ezra Pound, one of the most influential of the modern American poets and critics — and presented the theories of these critics to the members of the group, and their critical attitudes influenced the brief essays that Tate published in *The Fugitive*. This eclectic theory of poetry was first given full expression, however, in his essay "Poetry and the Absolute," published in the *Sewanee Review* of January 1927. Tate makes his critical position quite clear in that essay: he argues that all truth, including that by which one judges a work of art, is based on universal absolutes, principles that have always been valid and remain so under any circumstances. As a means of escaping the fallacy of subjective perception, which Tate believed was the only kind most modern men are capable of, man must search for his tradition. The "Ode to the Confederate Dead," which Tate began writing soon after completing this essay, presents with resounding emphasis the tragedy of a modern man cut off from his tradition, a tissue of beliefs, codes and attitudes through which he formerly had access to these universal truths.

In 1929, in France on a Guggenheim grant, Tate became even more aware of his cultural disorientation. The depth of his dejection is revealed in a poem written in 1929, entitled "Message from Abroad" and dedi-

---

Above (left): Walter Clyde Curry about 1935. *Below* (left): Merrill Moore in 1924. *Right:* William Frierson about 1925. *Photographs from Jesse E. Wills Collection.*

cated to Andrew Lytle. It opens with an epigraph from *Traveler to America* (1799): "Their faces were bony and sharp but very red." Tate makes it quite clear that his year in Europe has made the "red faces of his ancestors" less distinct in his memory, and he muses on the means by which tradition is passed from generation to generation. Some cultures, "Provence, / The Renascence, the age of Pericles," move clearly and distinctly through history and leave a lasting impression of their artistic theories and practices. Others—because they lack art and philosophy and because they never valued the rites, rituals, and ceremonies out of which a traditional order emerges—are mute and therefore are lost forever. As Professor M.E. Bradford has observed, Tate is stating a fundamental principle of his belief: "[T]he way of James and Joyce (the way followed by so many Americans in this decade) is rejected: aestheticism seen into and through." (Both Henry James, the American novelist, and James Joyce, the Irish poet and novelist, had argued that if the artist is to function at the height of his creative powers, he must sacrifice everything for art—home, family, country, and religion.) All of Tate's interest in tradition, its value and importance, clearly marked him as a southern writer. Because the southerner is the only American whose tradition was ruptured by an uncontrollable outside force, the Civil War, the southern writer is likely to feel the breach in the continuum of his tradition, the point at which it lost its aim and purpose. His northern counterpart will probably regard himself as a part of an unbroken tradition, a new man in a new world.

Although Tate continued to think of man's relation to his tradition, his attitude—because of his two years abroad, in 1928–29 and 1931–32, no doubt—shifted dramatically. He began to think of himself in relationship not to the southern tradition but to that of Western Europe. The impact of Spengler's philosophy again became paramount, and he began to note evidences of the deterioration of the moral fiber that had held Western European civilization together, as he earlier had become convinced of the lack of purpose in the American materialistic society. His *Poems, 1928–31* contained "Message from Abroad," ten "Sonnets of the Blood," and "The Cross." The sonnets dedicated to his brother Ben, who was well on his way toward earning a fortune in business, indicate the omnipresence of evil in human affairs, even in the most intimate details of the family heritage. "The Cross," according to R.K. Meiners, author of the first book-length study of Tate's artistic achievements, suggests that the life and resurrection of Jesus placed before man an intimation of immortality. From that time, therefore, "Like young wolves that have tasted blood," he can never satisfy his innermost desire. Man has been given a glimpse of immortality and can never again find complete nourishment in the physical details of the mortal world.

Although it seems unmistakable that Tate was moving toward religious certainty as a means of combating modern skepticism (modern man's tendency to doubt the validity of revealed religion) and positivism (the philosophic stance which argues that man can believe only that which may be verified by one or more of the five senses), his next collection of poems, *The Mediterranean and Other Poems* (1936), suggests that he is even more concerned about what is happening to the tradition that nurtured Christianity and allowed it to become a dominant point of view for two thousand years. In the title poem Tate contrasts the attitude that he and a group of his friends felt during a picnic at Cassis, a small village on the south coast of France, with the attitude that dominated Aeneas, the protagonist of Vergil's *Aeneid*. After the battle of Troy, with his father on his back, Aeneas had struggled to find a spot to settle and carry westward the Grecian civilization that had been destroyed. Tate and his friends had engaged in festive revelry, consuming sixty-one bottles of wine, along with tremendous quantities of coq au vin and many kinds of cheese. Aeneas and his group were so hungry that they were eating their food on slabs of bread when they realized that they were fulfilling a prophecy made by Anchises: he had proclaimed that when the explorers' hunger became so great, they would eat "their tables" they would know that their troubles were over because they had found a new home. According to this myth this was the means by which civilization had found a new station on its movement westward. It had moved from Greece to Rome. Tate compellingly contrasts the two groups of picnickers: "They, in a wine skin, bore earth's paradise," but "We've cracked the hemispheres with careless hand!" The meaning of the last statement becomes alarmingly clear in "Aeneas at Washington" when Tate imagines Aeneas's reaction to the capital city of America, the next center of the movement of civilization westward:

> I saw the thirsty dove
> In the glowing fields of Troy, hemp ripening
> And tawny corn, the thickening Blue Grass
> All lying rich forever in the green sun.
> I see all things apart, the towers that men
> Contrive I too contrived long, long ago.
> Now I demand little. The singular passion
> Abides its object and consumes desire

In the circling shadow of its appetite.
There was a time when the young eyes were slow,
Their flame steady beyond the firstling fire,
I stood in the rain, far from home at nightfall
By the Potomac, the great Dome lit the water,
The city my blood had built I knew no more
While the screech-owl whistled his new delight
Consecutively dark.

*Lines from "Aeneas at Washington" from COL-
LECTED POEMS by Allen Tate. Copyright ©
1952, 1953, 1970, 1977 by Allen Tate. Copyright
1931, 1932, 1937, 1948 by Charles Scribner's Sons.
Copyright renewed © 1959, 1960, 1965 by Allen
Tate. Reprinted by permission of Farrar, Straus
and Giroux, Inc.*

If modern man is to recover the sense of mission that once dominated
his life, he must turn his back on the material acquisitiveness that has
come to dominate America and retrace his steps, "make the journey
eastward," with the hope of rediscovering the natural human-rights theory upon which this country was founded and the principles of Christianity, which render to man a level of dignity he can know in no other
way. Allen Tate was well into his defense of religious humanism given in
I'll Take My Stand (1930) and moving toward the affirmation of Christian principles expressed in "Seasons of the Soul" (1944).

Although a native of Kentucky, Robert Penn Warren attended high
school and college in Tennessee and was an important member of all
three of the significant literary groups that Tennessee has contributed to
twentieth-century American literature. At Vanderbilt University, from
which he was graduated in 1925, he not only participated in the activities
of the Fugitive poets, but he profited much from his association with his
teachers, John Crowe Ransom and Donald Davidson, as well as from
that with his fellow student, Allen Tate. From the Fugitive meetings,
Warren recalled much later, he was convinced for the first time, although he had dabbled in verse before, "that poetry was a vital activity,
that it related to ideas, and to life." After he was graduated from Vanderbilt, *summa cum laude,* Warren entered the University of California
to earn a master's degree in English (1927). At Berkeley he was disap-
pointed to find his professors more interested in Marx and Engels than

Allen Tate in 1965. *Jesse E. Wills Collection.*

they were in Eliot and Pound. In the fall of 1927 he entered Yale to begin work on the Ph.D. in English. While he was at Yale, with the assistance of Allen Tate who was then in New York, Warren received a contract to do a biography of John Brown, the abolitionist who led an unsuccessful raid on the federal arsenal at Harper's Ferry in October 1859 as part of an involved and ill-conceived scheme to free the slaves.

This opportunity to become a professional writer, which Warren wanted above all else, distracted him from his work at Yale, and he put all of his energies into the writing of the biography, even to the point of going to Harper's Ferry to interview the sole surviving member of John Brown's raiding party. Like Tate's two biographies and Lytle's *Bedford Forrest and His Critter Company* (1931), Warren's *John Brown: The Making of a Martyr* (1929) is distinguished more for its author's ability to organize and present narrative detail than it is for its objective, factual accuracy. It does foreshadow to an amazing degree, as Charles H. Bohner observes in his informative study of Warren's literary career, Warren's future work as an outstanding novelist: "his ability to render a scene palpably and memorably, his insight into character, and his skill at wringing from a story every ounce of color and drama." The book is an amazing feat indeed when one considers its author was a young man of twenty-four who was supposed to have been fully engaged in the graduate program of Yale University.

In the fall of 1928 Warren entered Oxford University as a Rhodes scholar. There he was joined by another Vanderbilt alumnus, Cleanth Brooks of the class of 1928, and they laid the groundwork for their long and distinguished collaboration. At Oxford, Warren kept up his correspondence with Tate and renewed his acquaintance with Davidson and Ransom by visiting Nashville during his summers at home in Guthrie, Kentucky. He was fully informed, therefore, of the discussions that led to the publication of *I'll Take My Stand* (1930), to which he contributed an essay, "The Briar Patch." At Oxford, too, at the invitation of Paul Rosenfield, Warren wrote a long story, "Prime Leaf" (1931), the primary concern of which is the effect on a small boy of the arguments between his father and grandfather over the terroristic tactics of a group of "night riders" who were organized to resist the monopolistic practices of

Above: Ransom and Warren, February 27, 1973. *Photograph by Carswell Berlin. Below:* Robert Penn Warren in 1925, the year he joined the Fugitives. *Jesse E. Wills Collection.*

eastern tobacco buyers. The father's involvement leads to his shooting of one man and finally to his being murdered. Although Warren published other short stories during the 1930s — amid the time-consuming activities of teaching at Southwestern-at-Memphis, Vanderbilt, and Louisiana State, not to mention the founding and editing of the *Southern Review* and the publication of his first collaborative effort with Cleanth Brooks, *Understanding Poetry* (1938) — any reader of Warren's fiction can see that "Prime Leaf" figured prominently in his first novel, *Night Rider* (1939). In 1935, the year of the founding of the *Southern Review,* Warren published his first book of poems, *Thirty-six Poems,* which includes only one poem that had appeared in *The Fugitive,* "To a Face in a Crowd." Much of the poetry in this volume, unlike most of that published in later volumes, is traditional in form. Although the influence of Eliot is often too obvious, most of the poems are far superior to the juvenile verse Warren published as an undergraduate. The poetry in this collection, particularly the sequence "Kentucky Mountain Farm," reveals a keen awareness of the concrete particularities of a specific place. Many of the poems are concerned with themes that Warren has used many times since: the cycles of the seasons, time's eternal movement marked by the different generations of a single family, man's inability to know the nature of ultimate reality, one's responsibility for the repercussions of his personal decisions, his lost innocence, and his hope for redemption. With the publication of this collection of poems and his first novel, the literary career of one of the most versatile and distinguished men of letters of the twentieth century was firmly launched.

When John Crowe Ransom, in the December 1925 issue, announced that *The Fugitive* was suspending publication, he indicated that the poets would "continue to hold their regular meetings for the discussion of poetry and philosophy." Despite the best intentions of the members of the group, however, the "Fugitive experiment" as an organized activity was over. Although those left in Nashville did get together occasionally — especially when Tate, Warren, or some other member who had left town was visiting Nashville — the meetings became more and more irregular. Some of the members, like Davidson, who realized how significant the organized meetings at the Frank home were, began to conceive of

---

Five of Tennessee's best-known writers in 1956 — (left to right) Allen Tate, Merrill Moore, Robert Penn Warren, John Crowe Ransom, Donald Davidson. *The* Tennessean, *by Joe Rudis, photographer.*

projects that would hold the group together. At first someone suggested that the poets sponsor the publication of an anthology of the best poetry that had appeared in *The Fugitive*. This suggestion was not received too enthusiastically by some members of the group because they realized that much of their best work had not appeared in the journal. Then Tate suggested a collection of the best poetry written by the members of the group, regardless of when it was written and where it had first appeared. Davidson acted on this suggestion and collected a manuscript, and Tate, who was in New York at the time, after several refusals, persuaded Harcourt, Brace to publish the book.

Fugitive: An Anthology of Verse appeared on January 8, 1928, and looking through this volume today merely confirms the opinions expressed earlier: most of the Fugitives were entering new phases of their literary career. Ransom's best poetry had appeared in *The Fugitive;* now he was becoming more and more concerned with the considerable problem of attempting to formulate his theory of the nature and function of poetic discourse. Warren's mastery of the Eliot technique was becoming more apparent with each poem he published, and he was moving steadily toward the kind of poetry he would publish in *Thirty-six Poems* (1935). Tate's contributions to this volume included an early version of "Ode to the Confederate Dead"; and reading his later poems, those published after December 1925, one is immediately aware of the poet's increasing interest in the relationship between the artist and the tradition out of which he came. "Your whole showing is extremely powerful, not to say stunning," Davidson wrote Tate as soon as he had finished reading the volume. As much as Tate's poetic interests had expanded in two or three years, however, the kind of verse he was publishing had not changed as drastically as had that which Davidson was writing. In the same letter to Tate, Davidson explains his dissatisfaction with the kind of poetry he had published in *The Fugitive*. In the anthology he had included only "Fire on Belmont Street" from the poems he had written during the previous two years, the ones that would be included in *The Tall Men*. The others he had selected mainly from those he had done much earlier. "As for my own offerings," he wrote, "I am disgusted with them. They don't jibe at all, but fall into two crazy divisions, the Belmont Street thing warring against all the rest. Perhaps they are more indicative than I realize of my own confusion."

In "Fire on Belmont Street" one can see the nature of the concerns that will command the attention and absorb almost all of the creative energies of Ransom, Tate, and Davidson for the next ten years. (All three are moving toward their defense of certain basic southern attitudes, customs, and beliefs.) The enemy confronting the American citizen in modern times, Davidson insists, is vastly different from that which had formerly plagued him. He is not in danger of attacks by hostile Indians or the ravages of nature "red in tooth and claw." The present-day enemy is acquisitive materialism, whose power is suggested metaphorically as gigantic wheels rolling with "mass of iron / Against frail human fingers." No one has enough power, it seems, to "chain the dull / Gnaw of the fiery smoke, eternally settling into the beating heart." This enemy of uncontrolled industrialism, if no way is found to contain it, will feed on the citizens' "quick brains," their "beds," "homes," and "steeples." It will fill the veins of their children with fire that will curdle their blood and stop their weary pulse. The poet calls upon his reader to simplify his life, to "fly from the wrath of fire to the hills / Where the water is and the slow peace of time."

Between 1925 and 1928 some of the basic attitudes of the young poets who had declared in 1922 that they fled from nothing "faster than from the high caste Brahmins of the Old South" changed drastically. These altered attitudes affected the kind of writing they produced: for almost a decade after 1928, much of their effort was devoted to writing political, social, and cultural criticism, not to creating poetry and literary commentary. The particular event that motivated many of these young poets to look more critically and deeply into the tradition that produced them was the 1925 trial of John T. Scopes in Dayton, Tennessee, a young science teacher who had deliberately defied a Tennessee law that prohibited the teaching of evolution. Scopes's violation of the law was intended to test its constitutionality in the courts. The trial quickly turned into an international event because it was viewed as a direct confrontation between "revealed" fundamentalist religion and the truths demonstrated by modern science. It was covered by the national press, attracting such well-known journalists as H.L. Mencken. William Jennings Bryan assisted the prosecution to defend the authority of the Bible as the revelation of divine truth and the defense was headed by Clarence Darrow, who represented the position of the modern agnostic. Many years later Davidson recalled the effects of this trial on some of the Fugitives:

> I can hardly speak for others, but for John Ransom and myself, surely, the Dayton episode dramatized, more ominously than any other event easily could, how difficult it was to be a Southerner in the twentieth century, and how much more difficult to be a Southerner and also a writer. It was horrifying to see the cause of liberal education argued in

a Tennessee court by a famous agnostic lawyer from Illinois named Clarence Darrow. It was still more horrifying—and frightening—to realize that the South was being exposed to large scale public detraction and did not know or much care how to answer.

Reprinted from SOUTHERN WRITERS IN THE MODERN WORLD by permission of the University of Georgia Press © 1958 by The University of Georgia Press.

Obviously the young poets who a few years before had fled from nothing faster than "the high-caste Brahmins of the Old South" were soon to become involved in political, social, and economic controversy. They would not only defend the South, even with its fundamentalist beliefs, but they would mount an aggressive criticism of a culture too dependent upon acquisitive materialism.

3. The Agrarians

As Donald Davidson and John Crowe Ransom in amazement and disbelief observed, the picture of the South presented by the journalists covering the Scopes Trial, they were convinced that their section must be defended, as Davidson wrote later, "in historical terms as it was entitled to be defended." The two writers began to search for "some true and commanding image of the South" and for a means of stating the cultural conflict, which they thought to be worldwide. After years of writing and thinking, they brought together a group who shared their views, and in 1930, Twelve Southerners published an influential symposium entitled *I'll Take My Stand* in which the conflict was presented as one between Agrarianism and Industrialism. The publication of this book and related activity, including the composition of a second symposium, *Who Owns America?* (1936), resulted in the formation of a group that has since become referred to as the Nashville Agrarians.

Through correspondence with Tate, who was in France, Ransom and Davidson learned that Tate and Warren shared their concern and were eager to contribute ideas and essays in mounting a counterattack against those who were heaping "contempt and ridicule" on the South. On his own, Ransom undertook a defense of religious fundamentalism which he published as *God Without Thunder: An Unorthodox Defense of Orthodoxy* (1930). In this book Ransom argues for an inscrutable God, one that cannot be apprehended by the senses or comprehended by reason. He also published essays under such titles as "The South—Old or New?" and "The South Defends Its Heritage" in which he insists that the way of life in the antebellum South was the natural development of western European civilization and that that of the Northeast was an aberration. Only in the South was there appropriate emphasis both on the "economic forms" (the means of earning a livelihood, the use of applied science to improve man's standard of living) and the "aesthetic forms" (the amenities of life: customs, manners, rituals, ceremonies, religion, poetry, myth, familial and community loyalty and unity).

At the same time Davidson was offering his defense of the South by publishing in eastern periodicals his conviction that it was almost impossible to use southern materials in fiction and poetry without falling into the pattern established by the local colorists: southern people, manners, and customs can be used in fiction and poetry only if one concentrates upon the eccentric, the strange, and the bizarre, if one attempts to show that that strange land is unusual, if not unique. Davidson also began to encourage the residents of the South to move more cautiously in surrendering the elements of their native culture, to be certain that that which was adopted was superior to that which was abandoned.

In addition to keeping Tate and Warren aware of their activities, Ransom and Davidson were also discussing their ideas with some of their colleagues at Vanderbilt—John Donald Wade of the English department, Frank Lawrence Owsley of the history department, and Lyle Lanier of the psychology and philosophy department. Andrew Lytle, a graduate of Vanderbilt who had studied drama at Yale and acted briefly in New York before returning to live on the family plantation near Nashville, often joined these discussions. Almost all the members of the group were writing to friends who they thought would be interested in their cause.

The Agrarians were different from the Fugitives. In the first place only four members of the Fugitives—Ransom, Davidson, Tate, and Warren—joined the Agrarians. Most of the other Fugitives either had little interest in or were actively opposed to the activities of the Agrarians. The four Fugitives who formed the nucleus of the Agrarians attracted to them eight others—Andrew Lytle, John Donald Wade, Frank Lawrence Owsley, Herman Clarence Nixon, Lyle H. Lanier, Henry Blue Kline, John Gould Fletcher, and Stark Young. Although this group of men never held a meeting at which all of them were present—some of them never even met—together they brought out *I'll Take My Stand,* a book recently included among the twenty-five most influential upon the development of modern southern culture. It is, Davidson once wrote, "the most misunderstood, *unread* book" in American literature, and Professor Louis D. Rubin, Jr., who has edited two modern editions of the book now considered a classic, has pointed out that since its publication, it has been "a center of constant controversy," often condemned but never ignored.

Above: Frank L. Owsley, an Agrarian in the late 1940s. *Middle:* Lyle Lanier in 1930. *Below:* Henry B. Kline in 1930. *Photographs from Jesse E. Wills Collection.*

In 1930, when the book first appeared, however, its reception was mixed. It was favorably received by T.S. Eliot, John Peale Bishop, and others of literary stature, including William S. Knickerbocker, who wrote in the *Saturday Review of Literature* that it "was the most challenging book . . . since *Progress and Poverty*." Other reactions ranged from "a good antidote to the platitudes of progress" to "a high spot in the year's hilarity" and no one "can stem the tide of progress" or "reverse the movement of time." What most of the reviews of the books published then, and many of the reactions to it written since, reveal is that the intentions of its authors, as varied as they were, were grossly misunderstood. Not a single one of the twelve men who contributed to the symposium thought "time could be stopped" or the "clock turned back"; they were not searching for a Utopia—they did not believe imperfect men could ever effect a perfect social order. Neither were they so badly frightened by the presence of the black man and so uncertain of how they could dispose of him that they were incapable of confronting the genuine social and political issues of the day.

It is apparent, nevertheless, that the major contributors to *I'll Take My Stand* did not agree on what they hoped their communal efforts would achieve: Ransom wanted a society that placed equal emphasis on "aesthetic" and "economic" values, one in which poetry and the other arts were important means of communication. Davidson insisted that the modern American not sacrifice family and community loyalty, as well as his regional heritage, to a false god of progress. Lytle urged that an all-out effort be made in an attempt to preserve traditional folkways, legends, ballads, and the unique quality of life in the South. Allen Tate called for the return of religious humanism, and Robert Penn Warren feared the fate of the individual freedoms in a society dominated by materialism and pragmatism. At one point, however, as Professor Rubin, in his authoritative study of the movement, *The Wary Fugitive,* has pointed out, these widely ranging expectations came together and constituted a single aim:

> It was a way of striking out against the deifications of the machine, of warning against the depersonalizing forces of an unrestrained industrial capitalism. It was not Utopian so much as protest literature. The agrarian community which it imaged filled the function not of an economic alternative to the city, but a pastorale rebuke giving warning of the fragmenting complexity of modern urban society. And like all pastorale, it was written not for shepherds but for city dwellers— who already were living in urban America.

Like Thoreau in the century before, the Agrarians were warning their fellow Americans that they had been emphasizing the wrong values. Also like their New England predecessor, the southerners were many years ahead of some of their readers. As Thoreau was labelled a "skulker," a moral coward without the courage to face the problems inherent in living in the real world, for many years the Agrarians were called "academic idealists," "neo-Confederates," yearning for the restoration of a world that never existed. Only within the past few years — when the weaknesses of an economy based on planned obsolescence and the creation of false need through salesmanship and advertising, an economy too dependent upon the creation of a machine powered by an internal combustion engine which we no longer have the fuel to operate — when the deficiencies of some aspects of the American economic system have become so glaringly apparent — has the prophetic nature of the central argument of *I'll Take My Stand* become alarmingly clear. To many of the most perceptive readers of America — now when we cannot get clear air to breathe and uncontaminated food to eat — *I'll Take My Stand* is no longer a vague and sentimental book. To these readers it is now a profound assessment of our society; no longer are the book and its suggestions regarded as impractical; instead the promises made under the assumption of investing all of our resources in the applied sciences seem unrealistic. The energy shortage, among many other recent developments, makes our sprawling suburbs, our remote shopping centers, and our vast network of interstate highways seem impractical, if not downright absurd.

Most of the Agrarians were professional men of letters and were involved in many other literary activities while they were engaged in the defense of southern political, social, and cultural institutions. Between 1936, when he published his first novel (*The Long Night*), and 1957, when he brought out his last one (*The Velvet Horn*), for example, Andrew Lytle established a reputation, among a relatively few but completely devoted readers, as one of the most provocative and resourceful novelists of the century. Like William Faulkner, who never told two stories in the same way, Andrew Lytle is a remarkable innovator in his use of unusual and effective means of presenting the excellently structured and carefully controlled actions of his few novels and stories. His primary interest, it would seem, is in what he calls, in the only collection of his perceptive critical essays, *The Hero With the Private Parts* (1966), "the post of observation." Although Lytle's term is more complicated than the more commonly used "point of view" or "angle of narration," its function can best be understood in response to the questions, "whose story is being told?" and "by whom?" Which of the characters is most profoundly affected by the central action the author or his persona is relating? Two of Lytle's best short stories, both written in the mid-1930s, "Mr. MacGregor" and "Jericho, Jericho, Jericho," demonstrate his interest in angle of narration. Both are stories that truly represent the process through which Lytle, by devoting "unsparing attention to his craft," has transformed "it from merely that into art of a distinguished order." At his best, Lytle's art, Madison Jones, the contemporary Southern novelist, has pointed out, not only uses but uses up its subject and draws "the eye through the particular into the universal."

Lytle's attention to the form of fiction, as well as his omnipresent interest in the inevitable intertwinement of good and evil, innocence and experience, can be traced through all of his stories and novels. *The Long Night* (1936), set just before, during, and after the Civil War, is narrated by Lawrence McIvor, whose grandfather Cameron McIvor had been killed by a band of marauders and slave traders just before the outbreak of the Civil War. The story of violence and bloodshed, which Lawrence tells, was related to him one dark winter night by his Uncle Pleasant at his home in Winston County, Alabama. After his grandfather was killed, Lawrence learns, there is strong disagreement in the family as to what action it should take. William, Lawrence's father, wants to turn the whole matter over to the authorities and let justice be achieved by legal means. Pleasant's grief over his father's death is so profound, however, that he vows to track down all forty members of the gang and destroy them, thereby avenging his father's death. The story that Lawrence hears from his Uncle Pleasant is how this most improbable deed was accomplished despite obviously overwhelming obstacles, including the intervention of the Civil War.

One by one Pleasant tracks down and destroys those responsible for his father's murder. He kills secretly and alone, following some of his victims to Texas where they have fled attempting to evade him. Even after war is declared, Pleasant continues his personal vendetta. As Pleasant's grisly and obsessive plan draws closer and closer to completion, he finds his commitment beginning to waver. Finally he reaches the point where, when he has one of the enemy within his sights, he cannot pull the trigger. Like Colonel Sartoris in Faulkner's *The Unvanquished,*

Andrew Lytle, an Agrarian, about 1950. *Jesse E. Wills Collection.*

Pleasant has arrived at the point where he can spill no more human blood. Following the gruesome trail of reprisal, he has loved the dead too much and the living too little:

> Vengeance—the dark way. Into Shiloh woods he had gone, had carried it there. On that field where the living died and, dying, came more alive, he had lost it and had found himself. . . . Then suddenly he knew what he had done [as he stood by his friend's grave], what no man in this world may do. Twice he had loved—once the dead, once the living, and each by each was consumed and he was doomed.

Before beginning his harrowing tale of revenge and murder, of the omnipresence of human evil and the inability of man to stamp it out, Pleasant tells Lawrence: "I have brought you here for reasons unknown to anyone but myself. What I have to say is not a thing I can tell my wife and children. But it is a thing that must be told. And you are the next of kin." When the voice stops, after droning on "from sun to sun," the reader shares the narrator's feelings: "By degrees the steady fall of his words had beat all the warmth out of my senses, until terror crept over my body leaving it defenseless in the grip of rigid nerves. For hours my will had been the creature of that voice, rising and falling." The reader has learned with the narrator that "to be at home in the dark. To know what the long night meant. That was the secret of vengeance."

In this book, as in his other fiction, Lytle is reiterating at least two principles regarding the human situation. Man cannot live and function as a human being, capable of good and evil, love and hate, compassion and revulsion, outside the human community; and, too, any social order effected by man, despite its controlling, civilizing influences, will reflect the imperfections of its creators. The most persistent error the Americans have committed, Lytle argues, is in harboring the belief that some time in the future man will have corrected all of the injustices of his social order; then perfect men will live in a perfect society. All of man's problems, Lytle insists, cannot be solved by the political system. Lytle's essays, stories, and novels are offered as a direct refutation of what Professor R.W.B. Lewis, in his *The American Adam: Innocence, Tragedy, and Traditions in The Nineteenth Century,* one of the most perceptive studies available on the American cultural experience, calls the myth of the American Adam. Lewis describes this myth in this manner:

> The new habits to be engendered on the New American scene were suggested by the image of a radically new personality, the hero of the new adventure: an individual emancipated from history, happily

bereft of ancestry, untouched and undefiled by the usual inheritance of family and race; an individual standing alone, self-reliant and self-propelling, ready to confront whatever awaited him with the aid of his own unique and inherent resources. It is not surprising . . . that the new hero . . . was most easily identified with Adam before the Fall.

Reprinted by permission of The University of Chicago Press, copyright 1955.

Lytle, as Warren reiterates in "Original Sin," believes "nothing is lost, ever lost!" There will never be a "new innocence for us to be stayed by." In his unending search for archetypal experiences as subjects for his fiction, Lytle examines the loss of innocence, the initiation of youth into experience (thus into evil), in his story "The Mahogany Frame," a late story first published as "The Guide" in 1945. In "Alchemy" (1942), a well-structured sixty-page novella, closely related to and perhaps a sequel to *At the Moon's End* (1941), Lytle meditates on Spanish exploration in the New World and demonstrates, as Professor M.E. Bradford has noted, how "by sacrilegious means" one can reach "the condition of self-annointed god-head."

Man cannot rely upon his instincts, Lytle repeatedly reminds us, as a measure for his personal actions. Only by living as a member of a human community with individual actions and choices dominated by the rites, rituals, ceremonies, and customs of a civilized society, even with its obvious and inevitable defects, can man cope with the tensions, paradoxes, and ambiguities of an imperfect world.

Lytle's masterpiece is *The Velvet Horn,* surely the most underrated novel in modern American literature, one which Caroline Gordon thinks is a "landmark in American fiction, unique in its greatness and originality," if not in its complexity. In "The Working Novelist and the Mythmaking Process," a memorable essay on the writer's craft, Lytle explains the process by which he arrived at the controlling image in the novel — that of incest — one often misunderstood and misinterpreted. As he began to ponder the novel, Lytle writes, "I thought I wanted to do a long piece of fiction on a society that was dead. At the time I saw the scene as the kind of life which was the Southern version of a life that, discounting the sectional differences, had been common everywhere east of the Mississippi and east of the mountains. That life seemed to me to be what was left of the older and more civilized America, which as well retained the pattern of its European inheritance." His primary interest in the beginning, then, was to detail the disappearance of the sense of place and the dissolution of the family, two important landmarks in the destruction of our Christian heritage; he was seeking a myth which universally recurs on the human scene.

As his controlling idea was addressed by his creative imagination, he noted a shift of interest and intention. He began to conceive of his idea in universal terms; he realized, therefore, that the action portrayed in his fiction must be archetypal. As creative artist, he did not wish to make some comment about life; he wished to reconstitute reality itself. His novel was to be *about* the common mystery of life, mutability, represented in nature by seasonal change. As Faulkner has made abundantly clear, a real artist does not write about a society, but about people who happen to live under some kind of social agreement. As Lytle searched for an archetypal image to suggest man's frustrated attempt to return to the innocence and wholeness he had possessed before the Fall, he came upon brother-sister incest, a retelling of the Edenic myth in which Eve is taken from Adam's side. But the inherited code of the society to which Jack and Julie Cropleigh, two of the principal characters in the novel, belong does not permit such behavior—in the mundane world physical passion is a part of human love—so their son comes to know, as only great literature can teach him, the imperfections of human love, including as it must animal passion, and the impossibility of man's returning to his pristine state of innocence. Nowhere in modern fiction are the inexhaustible ambiguities of the human condition presented more forcefully.

Like the other Agrarians, Davidson's writing in the thirties was not confined completely to essays supporting the Agrarian cause. Although he did not write another book-length poem similar to *The Tall Men,* that poem set the tone and suggested the area of thematic concern of all the poems that he wrote until *The Long Street* (1961). In his next book, *Lee in the Mountains and Other Poems* (1938), he depicts with almost tragic intensity the crisis of modern times, the vacuum left by the disappearance of myth as a means of exploring ultimate reality. He portrays man in a dehumanized state, one in which he is almost completely dominated by glandular action and reaction. His researches into the past convinced him, he reiterated in essay after essay, that the Civil War, the first all-out, unrestrained war in history, was the line of demarcation separating the traditional, purposeful past from the aimless, chaotic present. As a consequence he began in the early 1930s "to compose a series of poems—largely narrative in character"—in which he attempted "to present some of the major figures of Southern history, at decisive or tragic moments in their careers." The book that finally evolved, however, *Lee in the*

Mountains and Other Poems contains poems on Lee, Jackson, and Forrest, but primarily this volume continues the protagonist's journey down "The Long Street," trying to go backward to the point where he can find his place in the tradition, and concludes that the disastrous Civil War was the destructive force that rendered the resourceful Tall Men of the frontier and The Confederate South impotent and hollow. Such was his obsessive theme in essay and poem until he published *The Long Street*. Although this book contains some poems dating from the twenties, those in the first section, "Northern Summers," written much later, reflect Davidson's reaction to his thirty-odd years of living each summer in Vermont. (He had first visited Vermont in the early thirties to serve on the faculty of the Bread Loaf School of English at Middlebury College. He and his family liked the climate there so well, not to mention the citizens of the community, that Davidson bought a home in Ripton, and he and his family spent their summers there until he died. His most often anthologized essay, "Still Rebels, Still Yankees," gives irrefutable proof of his deep affection for Vermont and its inhabitants.) These Vermont poems demonstrate the poet's sure ear for sound, his deep knowledge of classical literature, and his enviable ability to write simple, straightforward, yet elegant, dignified and uncluttered blank-verse lines. They are, nevertheless, no less rhetorical than the earlier poems. The poet is still less concerned with the undiluted transfer of intense feeling and sincere emotion than he is in stating a specific attitude or a firmly held point of view.

There is no question, however, that Davidson's compelling interest during this period, as it was for the remainder of his life, was defending the principle of the necessity of maintaining sectional integrity in America, both Rebel and Yankee. Writing in 1957 Davidson comments on what the Agrarian movement had meant to him and what he thought had accrued to his friends because of their participation in it: "Our total purpose was to seek the image of the South which we could cherish with high conviction and to give it, wherever we could, the finality of art in those forms, fictional, poetical or dramatic, that have the character of myth and therefore, resting on belief, secure belief in others, and, unlike arguments, are unanswerable, are in themselves fulfilled and complete. Such was the total purpose, of which the so-called 'Agrarian' movement was but a declaratory preface."

Davidson was convinced, in his words, that only "honor, truth, imagination, human dignity, and limited acquisitiveness" could provide an adequate foundation for a lasting order. That his commitment to these principles was total and permanent is demonstrated by the fact that all of his writing from 1930 until his death, both essay and poem, reiterate this credo. During the thirties, in addition to contributing an essay, "That This Nation May Endure: the Need for Political Regionalism," to the second Agrarian symposium *Who Owns America?*, he published more than three dozen articles in magazines of national circulation defending the autonomy of the southern region. Even the poetry he wrote during this period, with the exception of "Lee in the Mountains," hovers dangerously near didacticism—that is, it attempts to persuade us to accept the author's view of the subject under consideration—and his widely adopted and extremely useful textbook, *American Composition and Rhetoric* (1939), effectively employs numerous examples to demonstrate the validity of Southern attitudes, manners, customs, and beliefs.

Ransom's dedication to the Agrarian cause was not as absorbing as Davidson's, although he spent most of 1930–32 writing a treatise on economics. When the book was refused by *Harper's,* he published one essay from it "Land! An Answer to the Unemployment Problem," which argues that many of the unemployed urban dwellers should be resettled on the land at government expense. Then he destroyed the manuscript. Although he devoted most of his time and energy to the development of his influential theories on the nature and function of poetry, which would be published in *The World's Body* (1938), he did contribute "What Does the South Want?" to *Who Owns America?*. Ten of the three dozen or so essays he published in the 1930s also definitely support Agrarianism. By 1937, however, one can find ample evidence to demonstrate that Ransom's interest in the movement was waning. In his letter of June 8, 1937, to Edwin Mims, chairman of the Vanderbilt English department, indicating his reasons for believing his move from Vanderbilt to Kenyon would advance his literary career, he wrote that if the kind of writing he proposed to do was on "regionalism or agrarianism, I would be going into foreign parts. But I have about contributed all I have to those movements and I have of late gone almost completely into literary work." The previous year he had indicated his Agrarian concerns were inhibiting his attempts to get back to theoretical literary criticism. In a review written a few years after arriving in Ohio in the autumn of 1937, he chastises W.P. Southard for proposing "to found an agrarian community within which innocence may be recovered" and insists that a

---

John Crowe Ransom in 1930. *Jesse E. Wills Collection.*

modern industrial society is a part of the post-scientific world that man must accept. The Potsdam declaration, he wrote, was an attempt by the Allies of World War II to dismantle the German military and industrial complex and destroy that nation's means of prosecuting another war. The agrarian economy that would result from such an act would once have been very pleasing to Ransom, but he now regarded the action as "heavy punishment," although he had earlier believed such a sentence would have brought "greater happiness to the people." After this public statement of his position, Davidson proclaimed in a letter to Tate that on other occasions Ransom had "swung an axe widely, not much regarding his friends."

Although, as we have seen, Tate published an important collection of poems, *The Mediterranean and Other Poems,* in which he announced his intentions of seeking a broader cultural heritage than that which had been conceived by some of his Nashville friends, his severance from the movement was not as direct and final as that of Ransom. After all, as he had said all along, his major objective in joining the Agrarians was to remind his readers of the urgent need for a return to religious humanism. With Herbert Agar, therefore, he edited the second Agrarian symposium, *Who Owns America?, A New Declaration of Independence,* to which he contributed an essay, "Notes on Liberty and Property." During the thirties, too, he published his first *Selected Poems* (1937), and his only novel, *The Fathers* (1938); in the latter he declared that the absence of an appropriate religion in the Old South was a major flaw in the antebellum society. The first collection of his essays, *Reason in Madness: Critical Essays* (1941) contains only two essays which may in any way be interpreted to support the Agrarian position: "Liberalism and Tradition" and "What Is a Traditional Society?" Obviously Tate's commitment to the Southern tradition was not as compelling as Davidson's; in fact in the mid-forties he wrote a brief note overtly critical of his old friend's attitude toward the position of the black man in contemporary society. Although Warren contributed "Literature as a Symptom," to *Who Owns America?* — one of the best essays in the collection — the brilliant critical assessment of Sidney Lanier entitled "The Blind Poet: Sidney Lanier," "Some Don'ts for Literary Regionalists," and a few other essays that may be used to defend the fundamental issues supported by the Agrarians, his relationship with that group in the thirties, as it had been with the Fugitives in the twenties, was peripheral.

Not all Tennessee writers of the thirties, however, were associated with the Agrarians, although that movement attracted many of the most significant. One of the most interesting and talented writers of the time was Evelyn Scott, who was born in Clarksville, Tennessee, on January 17, 1893. (Her real name was Elsie Dunn.) A precocious child, she began writing fiction at the age of nine and published her first story at thirteen. On December 26, 1913, just a few weeks before she was twenty-one, she eloped with a member of the Tulane University faculty, while she was in school at Sophie Newcomb College and Art School.

Because the two never married and Miss Dunn knew a common-law arrangement would be considered scandalous by her family and friends, she and her lover, F.C. Wellman, changed their names to Cyril K. and Evelyn Scott. Her desperately lonely and poverty-stricken years in Brazil are evocatively presented in her unusual autobiography *Escapade* (1923). Although she lived her early adult years in the pioneer society of an undeveloped South American country, one in which few authors existed—none were among her acquaintances, and books were almost impossible to obtain—Evelyn Scott's interest in writing never waned. Working in almost complete aesthetic and intellectual isolation, she employed in her writing such modernistic techniques as stream of consciousness, impressionism, and symbolic realism.

In addition to her autobiography, she published poetry in *Poetry, Dial,* and the *Egotist.* She was the author of at least a half dozen novels, the best known of which, perhaps, is *The Wave* (1929). A sensitive and perceptive reader, she was also a good critic, and her essay on Faulkner's *The Sound and the Fury* was one of the first to point out the reasons why that book is now considered one of the greatest in American literature. Her respectable literary reputation quickly dissipated after about 1937, perhaps because of a scathing attack on communism, which she published in that year. At any rate, she published nothing after 1941, and when she died in New York in 1963, she left a considerable body of work in manuscript form, some of which is considered among her best writings.

Another Tennessee writer who acquired a considerable reputation in the 1930s was Harry Harrison Kroll. Although he was born near Kokomo, Indiana, on February 18, 1888, he spent his boyhood on farms near Dyersburg, Tennessee. Kroll was graduated from George Peabody College for Teachers in 1923 and earned his master of arts degree from the same institution two years later. In 1926 he began a distinguished teaching career at Lincoln Memorial University, where he taught both Jesse Stuart and James Still. From Lincoln Memorial he moved to the University of Tennessee at Martin, where he remained until he retired in 1960.

Although Kroll published more than a dozen novels, beginning with *The Mountainy Singer* (1928) and concluding with *Blue Grass, Belles, Bourbon* (1967), the peak of his literary reputation came with *Cabin in the Cotton* (1931), his third book. A realistic portrayal of life on a southern farm, this novel became a regional best seller. At his death in 1967, Kroll left four novels and numerous short stories unpublished.

Perhaps best known as the wife of Allen Tate, Caroline Gordon is a novelist and short story writer of undeniable talent, a significant literary critic, and a resourceful and stimulating teacher of creative writing. Born in Todd County, Kentucky, she was graduated from Bethany College in West Virginia in 1916. After her graduation she taught in high school for three years before accepting a post as reporter for the *Chattanooga News* in 1920. During her tenure with that paper she wrote one of the earliest serious assessments of the Fugitive poets. This essay made her name known to Allen Tate, even before he actually met her, while he was visiting Robert Penn Warren during the summer of 1924. The young couple fell in love and married a few months later. The marriage ended in divorce thirty-five years later.

The Tates lived in Tennessee for many years on several different occasions. Her first novel, *Penhally,* was published in 1931. Since then she has published eight other novels, an anthology of short fiction (with Allen Tate), a critical book entitled *How to Read a Novel* (1957), and two collections of short stories. Her best known books are *Aleck Maury, Sportsman* (1934), based on the life of her father, James Morris Gordon; *The Strange Children* (1951), in which she recreates her life near Clarksville, Tennessee, from 1930 to 1938; and *The Malefactors* (1956), which includes an assessment of many of the members of her literary generation. Her artistic discipline and her broad range of vision, as well as her mastery of the craft of fiction, is best revealed, many critics believe, in her two collections of short stories: *The Forest of the South* (1945) and *Old Red and Other Stories* (1963). In addition to these superb short stories and the novels previously mentioned, Miss Gordon is the author of other books of unquestioned excellence: *None Shall Look Back* (1937), a novel of the Civil War, and *Green Centuries* (1941), a serious historical study of the settlement of Kentucky.

By the late 1930s Agrarianism as an organized group effort was no

---

Above: Evelyn Scott at Sophie Newcomb College. *Below:* Scott as a child. *Photographs courtesy of Robert Welker.*

longer active, although many of the members of the group—Davidson, Owsley, and Lytle, particularly—continued to embrace publicly, especially in their writings, the principles on which *I'll Take My Stand* was based. Today, fifty years after that book was published, its reputation is higher, perhaps, than it has been at any other time in its history. Its contributors, who were usually referred to as reactionaries, now are often called prophets.

In 1937, however, Ransom published an essay entitled "Criticism, Inc.," in which he proclaimed that literary criticism must become "more scientific, or precise . . . it must be developed by the collective and sustained effort of learned persons." The next year he argued in *The World's Body* that poetry can reveal that which one cannot know otherwise. If poetry, or any other literary activity, is to reveal the unique quality of knowledge it possesses, it must be read as literature and not as biography, history, philosophy, theology, or anything else. The manner in which Ransom was insisting that literature should be studied, some of his former students well knew, was the way it had been read and discussed in his classes. Ransom was issuing a challenge which was immediately taken up by Tate, Warren, and Cleanth Brooks, another of Ransom's students, and that movement which we now call the New Criticism was underway.

4. The Southern New Critics

As early as the spring of 1914 John Crowe Ransom was giving some attention to a book on aesthetics. Particularly he wished to define clearly how poetry differs from prose and precisely what poetry can accomplish, because of these differences, that prose cannot. From Lakeville, Connecticut, where he was teaching Latin, he wrote to his father on February 4, 1914, that he was convinced that the "imaginative mode rather than the logical mode is . . . precisely what the exigencies of meter" might induce in a poetic composition. Because "words have a double nature" — that is, they "stand for things and are associated inseparably with thought" — they have a "second value," which he would later call texture. The poet "*has* to use words . . . which fail of precision and introduce extraneous color and distract the attention and suggest beautiful enterprises of the imagination."

Any reader of Ransom's criticism will recognize in this early tentative statement the rudiments of the description of the unique nature of poetry included in his essay "Wanted: An Ontological Critic," written nearly thirty years later: "But it is hard to say what poetry intends by its odd structure. What is the value of a structure which (a) is not so tight and precise on its logical side as a scientific prose structure generally is; and (b) imports and carries along a great deal of foreign matter which is clearly not structural but even obstructive?" This "loose logical structure" always found in combination with this "irrelevant local texture" makes the nature of poetic composition unique. Although a poem always has the basic structure of any "logical discourse" — this is the part of the poem which may be converted into a prose paraphrase — it also has an "irrelevant texture," which includes diction, imagery, sound, and metaphor. This textural element cannot be expressed in prose, and this fact makes the poetic composition different from scientific discourse.

In a series of brief critical pieces he contributed to *The Fugitive* Ransom concerned himself with problems confronting the poet who must try to conform to a predetermined pattern of sound (meter and perhaps rhyme) and at the same time develop a logical argument. Trying to accomplish this two-fold intention, he was convinced, led some modern poets into the obscure and esoteric. Too many modern readers associate the English literary tradition with the Romantic and Victorian poets—from Wordsworth and Shelley to Tennyson and Arnold—and they expect wisdom "to come from the mouths of babes."

In an attempt to convince modern readers that they must accept poetry that represents the age in which they live, thus a post-scientific poetry, and one that will command all their faculties, Ransom took a year's leave of absence from teaching during the academic year of 1926–27 to compose a book-length treatise on the nature and function of poetry. After more than two years of hard work, he completed a draft of this proposal, which he called "The Third Moment," and submitted it to a publisher. When it was rejected, he burned the manuscript; therefore the only way we can determine the burden of Ransom's argument is through a series of letters he wrote Allen Tate during the time he was writing the manuscript. On September 5, 1926, Ransom outlined in detail the plan for the proposed book:

> The three moments in the historical order of experience are as following:
> 1. The first moment is the original experience—pure of all intellectual content, unreflective, concrete, and singular. . . .
> 2. The moment after. . . . In the second moment cognition takes place. . . . The feature of the second moment is that it is now that the record must be taken of the first moment that has just transpired. This record proceeds inevitably by way of *concepts* discovered in cognition. It is the beginning of science. Its ends are practical but its means are abstractions; subtractions from the whole. . . . So experience becomes History, conceptualized knowledge. . . .
> 3. We become aware of the deficiency of the record. Most of experience is . . . missing from it. All our concepts and all our histories put together cannot add up to the wholeness with which we started out. . . . How can we get back to that first moment? There is only one answer: By images. The Imagination . . . brings out the original experience.

When man makes images in an attempt to reconstitute what he once knew, he cannot quite succeed, because the second moment—the period of logical cognition—has interceded. The images created in the first moment are now mixed with concepts or ideas. The initial experience is perceptual, but in the second moment concepts are formed by concentrating only on those aspects of the original experience that will permit us to make some abstract statement about it. This is the time in which the scientist, the social scientist, and the theologian do their important work. The third moment is the time in which the poet attempts with his creative imagination to recreate the first moment in which what he knew was purely perceptual, consisting of images only. He is attempting to perform his basic function, to reconstitute reality. Since the second moment has intervened, however, the poet cannot recreate his vision of reality through images only; this pure perceptual view has been adulterated by concepts. His view of reality is now composed of images and ideas. (The modern poet is a post-scientific man. He *thinks* and *senses;* therefore his poetry must be composed of both images and ideas, or in Ransom's terms, of structure and texture.)

This theory of the nature and function of poetry is given its fullest treatment in Ransom's essay, "Poetry: A Note in Ontology," included in *The World's Body* (1938). He classifies poetry into three types: physical, Platonic, and metaphysical. The first of these he calls genuine poetry because it attempts to present "things in their thingness." The best example of a twentieth-century group who have attempted to produce physical poetry, he writes, were the Imagists. An outstanding example of this kind of verse is Amy Lowell's "Thompson's Lunch Room, Grand Central Station":

> Jagged greenwhite bowls of pressed glass
> Rearing snow-peaks of chipped sugar
> Above the lighthouse-shaped castors
> Of gray pepper and gray-white salt.

Although physical poetry is concerned with "the basic constituent" of all verse—images—it is only "half-poetry" because, since all concepts—"ideas"—are scrupulously excluded, it possesses no emotional or intellectual content. It is all texture and no structure.

The second classification of poetry, Platonic, he immediately labels bogus poetry because, he says, the writers of this kind of verse have no faith in images. They merely use them to illustrate ideas. To demonstrate his meaning he quotes from "Pippa Passes" by Robert Browning:

> The year's at the spring
> And day's at the morn;
> Morning's at seven;

> The hill-side's dew-pearled;
> The lark's on the wing;
> The snail's on the thorn:
> God's in his heaven —
> All's right with the world!

Then Ransom expresses his objection to this much quoted lyric: This "is a piece of transparent homiletics; for in it six pretty, coordinate images are marched, like six little lambs to the slaughter, to a colon and a powerful text."

The third classification, which Ransom calls "metaphysical poetry," he names true poetry. True poetry has both structure and texture, idea and image because it is built upon a central figure, a "metaphor that is meant." It is "meant" because it is "developed so literally that it must be meant, or predicated so baldly that nothing else can be meant." Through a combination of image and idea, structure and texture, this fully developed metaphor presents an identity between two objects, which "is partial, though it should be considerable, and proceeds to an identification which is complete." To demonstrate what he means by true poetry he quotes a portion of a poem by the seventeenth-century poet Abraham Cowley:

> Oh take my Heart, and by that means you'll prove
>   Within, too stor'd enough of love:
> Give me but yours, I'll by that change so thrive
>   That Love in all my parts shall live.
> So powerful is this my change, it render can,
> My outside Woman, and your inside Man.

Although the poet is saying that he and his mistress have exchanged hearts, the statement is obviously not to be taken literally. "What has actually been exchanged," Ransom reminds us, "is affections, and affections are only in a limited sense the same as hearts. Hearts are unlike affections in being engines that pump blood and form body; and it is a miracle if the poet represents the lady's affections as rendering her inner being into man." But he succeeds, "with this mixture, in depositing with us the image of a very powerful affection."

In a series of critical essays, therefore, Ransom developed a theory which argues that literature functions as a means of cognition, a theory that came to be referred to as one that insists that literature is an important source of a specific kind of knowledge. As his friend Allen Tate expressed it, "[I]n the poem we get knowledge of a whole object, . . .

complete knowledge, the full body of the experience. . . . However we may see the completeness of poetry, it is a problem less to be preserved."

In his classes at Vanderbilt, as well as in the meetings of the Fugitives, Ransom had been insisting that poetry of the right kind is the means by which "we must know what we have arranged that we shall not know otherwise." This kind of poetry does not wish to "idealize the world"; it wishes to "realize the world, to see it better," to restore to the world of experience its "body and solid substance."

One of the students whom Ransom had influenced most — and who in turn had assisted Ransom most as he attempted to articulate his theories of the nature and function of poetry — was Allen Tate. In a very early essay — "Whose Ox," *The Fugitive* (December 1922) — Tate had argued against the commonly held opinion that poetry "must *represent* some phase of life ordinarily perceived" and that the poet must "look for his effects in a new combination of images representing only the constituted material world." Instead, he insisted, poets may be able to achieve the desired effect only by "rearranging" or "remaking, remolding, in a subjective order, the stuff they must necessarily work with — the material world." Although this essay clearly shows the influence of Tate's acquaintance with the literary theories and practices of the Symbolists, it reveals, too, his desire to find a means of synthesizing traditionalism with modernism. Although T.S. Eliot has clearly illuminated, Tate argued, the path that modern poetry will take, there are many poets "still faithful to the older, if not more authentic tradition."

One can see in Tate's deliberations here considerations of the unique nature of the poetic composition, ponderings of the sort that led Ransom to his famous "texture-structure formulation" as a means of retaining the traditional elements of verse and at the same time incorporating into the poem the most effective of modernistic techniques. In two essays, written in the late thirties and early forties, Tate demonstrates the similarities between his literary theories and those of Ransom. These essays serve as a perfect gloss on Ransom's statement in the opening pages of *The World's Body*: "I am most under obligations to Mr. Allen Tate, with whom I have been in close communication, and whose views of poetry I share, so far as I know them, with fewest and slightest reservations. Between us, when the talk was at a certain temperature, I have seen observations come to the surface in a manner to illustrate the theory of anonymous or communal authorship."

In the first of these essays, "Tension in Poetry," Tate insists that poets are less interested in making the reader's response to the poem logical and orderly than they are in arousing a definite response. (As Ransom argued, the poet intends to reconstitute reality, not to make some comment about it.) What Ransom has labeled "structure" and "texture," in poetry, Tate refers to as "extensive" and "intensive" meaning. The poet primarily interested in structure (the traditionalist), one who is trying to pattern a logical argument, "begins at or near the denotative end of the line"; that is, he is primarily concerned with the accepted dictionary definition of the words he uses. The symbolist poet (the modernist), one primarily concerned with texture, begins at the other, the intensive end. Each "by a straining feat of the imagination tries to push his meaning as far as he can toward the opposite end, so as to occupy the whole scale." Tate is suggesting that the modern poet is more interested in the meaning the word suggests to the reader than he is in what the word explicitly names or describes. The reaction of these two conflicting forces, what Ransom calls the impact of texture on structure, gives the poem its unique meaning.

That modern man must get from poetry a quality of knowledge available nowhere else is a result of the impact of positivism on contemporary thought. Positivism diverts our attention from the concrete particularities of the actual world by concentrating on the abstract process by which knowledge is acquired, by insisting we can know nothing except that which can be verified by one or more of the five senses. One of the first betrayers of poetry, Tate says in "Literature as Knowledge," was Matthew Arnold, the nineteenth-century English writer, who extended "the hand of fellowship to the scientist." Early in the present century I.A. Richards, one of the most influential contemporary critics, surrendered to the positivists in relegating the significance of poetry to a "mere readiness for action," rather than finding in poetic thought "action" itself. The concrete result of this mass defection is that the readers of poetry, the few who are left, have come to think of themselves merely as passive recipients. Poetry in these readers' opinion is not expected to move them to a significant action or reveal to them a fundamental truth. Because the reading of poetry in the present day is not considered an activity of the first order, little attempt is made by the professional educator to assist the student in discovering in literature that quality of knowledge that exists almost nowhere else. The basic reason the teacher cannot aid the student in deriving from literature the unique knowledge it contains, as Ransom pointed out in "Criticism, Inc.," is that the secondary or college teacher of literature does not know how to deal with his subject. Professors of English may be learned, but they are not "critical" men. They may know the "data of literature," but they do not feel an obligation to commit themselves to a literary judgment. Although they may have acquired a great deal of information about the author of a literary work, the genre to which the work belongs, or the age in which it was written, they know little about the work itself. Since they do not know how to read literature, they can offer little assistance to their students in acquiring this essential skill.

In this campaign to restore poetry to its rightful place of honor, Ransom and Tate were joined by two of their old friends, Cleanth Brooks and Robert Penn Warren. In 1939, the year following Ransom's publication of *The World's Body* and during the time in which Tate was writing some of his most influential essays, Brooks brought out *Modern Poetry and the Tradition*. In this influential work, he introduces his discussion of modern poetry with a statement of purpose: He hopes, he says, to assist those readers, whose "conception of poetry is . . . primarily defined . . . by the achievement of the Romantic Poets," to understand and appreciate the poetry of their own age. Although he admits that the work of many modern poets is often obscure, and sometimes even esoteric, it is significant and never incomprehensible. To find the tradition in which these modern poets are working one must go beyond the poets of the eighteenth and nineteenth centuries, back to the seventeenth century masters. Only among this latter group will one discover the "conception of the metaphor" used by the best of the twentieth-century poets. Like their seventeenth-century predecessors, the modern poets consider their proper role as that of maker, of reconstituting experience through appropriately blending intellect and emotion. With Ransom, Brooks thinks one must go back to the seventeenth century to find poets who, like their modern counterparts, do not oversimplify experience by omitting from it all opposing and discordant elements. The modern poet follows the example of the metaphysicals in attempting to resolve these seemingly contradictory elements into a larger unity.

Although the similarities between Brooks' literary theories and those of Ransom are many, there are points at which, as Ransom once stated, there is also "a little divergence." Brooks feared that Ransom's division of a poem into a "logical structure" and an "irrelevant texture" might lead to a false conflict between content and form. A prose paraphrase, Brooks insists, merely serves as a kind of scaffolding from which one may look over a poem and observe its myriad details; it is neither the poem itself nor a "rack on which the stuff of a poem is hung." Ransom retaliates by observing that in refusing to recognize the functional pur-

pose of a poem's structure, a critic like Brooks "goes straight from one detail to another in the manner of the bee who gathers honey from the several blossoms as he comes to them, without noticing the bush that supports all the blossoms."

Their differing views on how a poem is unified leads to their making different demands upon the metaphor. Ransom insisted upon a single and consistent development of the figure; for only in a tightly structured, strictly unified, and fully developed metaphor can the poet show the procedure through which a slight similarity between two objects becomes an "identification which is complete." Brooks, on the other hand, allows some "emotive meanderings" as long as these seeming digressions contribute to the poem's tone. Unlike Ransom, Brooks argues that the coherence of a poem depends not on its "ideational core," but on the development of its dominant metaphor through a series of "resolved stresses." These differences obviously were not irreconcilable. Both critics believed poetry to be an activity central to civilized behavior; consequently the best minds of any generation should be concerned with its creation and reception. Ransom devoted much time and energy in an effort to persuade readers that poetry is essential because it contains a quality of knowledge one can obtain almost nowhere else. Brooks, whom Ransom once identified as the "best reader of difficult poetry alive," demonstrated in essay, explication, and public address how these truths may be discovered and used.

In 1938, Ransom was calling for a professional corps of critics to deal formally with the kind of "knowledge by which we must know what we have arranged that we shall not know otherwise," that unique "individual object which tends to be universalized, but is not permitted to suffer this fate." In that same year Cleanth Brooks and Robert Penn Warren published *Understanding Poetry,* a widely used textbook that in the next twenty years would go through four large editions and revolutionize the way poetry was taught in the classroom. The aim of this influential book was quite simple; it attempted to demonstrate that if the poem is to reveal the unique quality of knowledge it contains, it must be read as poetry and not as something else. The three most common substitutes for

---

Above: John Crowe Ransom in 1939. *Photograph courtesy of Robb Reavill Ransom. Below:* Some of the Southern New Critics, May 5, 1956 —(left to right) Allen Tate, Cleanth Brooks, Robert Penn Warren. *Jesse E. Wills Collection.*

poetry, the editors point out in a "Letter to the Teacher," are "1. Para-phrase of logical or narrative content; 2. Study of biographical and his-torical materials; 3. Inspirational and didactic interpretation." Although paraphrase is useful and may be even necessary in the preliminary read-ing of a poem, and a knowledge of the author's life and the times in which he lived may aid in its interpretation, these must be used as "means" and not as "literary constructs," not as an historical or ethical doctrine. They are means to aid the reader in discovering the meaning of a poem and should not be substituted for the poem itself.

What these authors are trying to avoid is the kind of activity Ransom says is demanding most attention in the classroom in which literature is supposed to be taught. The students in many classes devoted to the study of Romantic poetry, Brooks and Warren fear, expend too much in-tellectual energy attempting to find the answers to such questions as: Ex-actly what kind of affliction did Byron suffer? Did he have a club foot? If so, which foot was affected? What was the color of Keats's hair? Why are there so many differing descriptions of its precise shade—from sandy to fiery red—among Keats's friends, acquaintances, and contem-poraries? How did Coleridge and Wordsworth's friendship affect each other's work? Too often, they insist, students spend their class and study time attempting to find the answers to such fascinating and absorbing biographical questions and discover later, some of them, that these poets wrote a considerable amount of very good poetry.

Most college textbooks, these editors continue, add to the confusion and suggest at best a vague, impressionistic interpretation of a poem. They give a few examples of the kind of questions appearing in some of the most widely used texts. One book gives only one comment after Keats's "Ode to a Nightingale": "The song of the nightingale brings sad-ness and exhilaration to the poet and makes him long to be lifted up and away from the limitations of life. The seventh stanza is particularly beautiful." But if this poem is to be read as a meaningful cognitive expe-rience, Brooks and Warren insist, the reader must be concerned with matters such as the following: "1. How is the paradox of 'exhilaration' and 'sadness' related to the theme of the poem? . . . 2. The seventh stanza is referred to as 'beautiful,' but on what grounds is the student to take any piece of poetry as 'beautiful?' 3. Even if the exercise quoted is relevant, there is a real danger that the suggestion to the student to look for the beautiful in the poem will tend to make him confuse with poetic excellence the mention of beautiful or agreeable objects."

The editors of *Understanding Poetry* state the aims of their approach explicitly and exactly: "1. Emphasis should be kept on the poem as a poem. 2. The treatment should be concrete and inductive. 3. A poem should be treated as an organic system of relationships, and the poetic quality should never be understood as inhering in one or more factors taken in isolation."

Such a tightly structured and organically arranged selection of verse, complemented by a series of tightly focused, inductively argued explanations of many of the poems, had never before been placed in the hands of students. Fully realizing that the teachers were little better prepared than their students to study verse in the manner proposed by this book, the editors explained the purpose of its organization with care and in detail. They begin with the simplest kind of verse and demonstrate how the reading of a poem should differ from that of prose fiction. Then in a logical and consistent manner they point out through examples exactly how the poet attempts to provoke the desired response. Finally there is a discussion of such poetic devises as imagery, diction, figurative language, rhyme, rhythm, and meter.

Following this forthright discussion is a selection of more than two hundred poems and fifty analyses of individual poems. Most of these analyses are lengthy and detailed; they are always focused directly upon the poem — its form, language, metrical devises, stanzas, rhyme and similar matters — and the treatment of the poetry, as promised, is always "concrete and inductive."

Never before had the student and his teacher had available in easy, accessible form so much of the material essential to their becoming aware of the cognitive function of literature. Seldom, if ever, before in his study of literature had the student been so constantly and persuasively encouraged to search out the unique qualities of the art object or the manifold compensations of such a study. A careful reading of this text not only will teach a student much about the nature and function of poetry, but it will help him to understand why so many of John Crowe Ransom's own students have attested to the profound effect his teaching had upon them. One can readily understand how stimulating and informative those discussions at the James M. Frank home must have been on the young poets assembled there. As Hugh Kenner, a significant and influential commentator on modern literature, has pointed out, "No man, it is possible to say, has had more effect on the way the subtler operations of language are comprehended in this country in this century. There is probably not a freshman in the United States whose experience of the English survey . . . is not in large part traceable to concerns of

Ransom's. It makes no difference that he has never heard of Ransom."
Surely *Understanding Poetry* has had a more profound effect on the
teaching of poetry than any other book ever published in America.

As any reader of modern American literature is aware, however, Robert Penn Warren did not devote all of his creative energy during the thirties and forties to textbooks demonstrating how literature should be
read. One of the most gifted, versatile, and broadly appreciated authors
of the twentieth century, he was writing some of those books of poetry,
fiction, and literary criticism that have earned for him every important
literary award except the Nobel Prize. Equally adept, apparently, in fiction, poetry, and non-fiction prose, Warren has few competitors—one
can think only of Edmund Wilson and Allen Tate as serious challengers
—for the title of American man of letters of the twentieth century. In addition to such profoundly influential theoretical and speculative critical
essays as "Pure and Impure Poetry" (1942), and "Knowledge and the
Image of Man" (1955), during the nineteen forties and fifties Warren
wrote influential, interpretative essays on a broad range of English and
American writers from Coleridge, Faulkner, and John Crowe Ransom
to Eudora Welty, Katherine Anne Porter, and Peter Taylor. He was also
co-editor of such widely used textbooks as *An Approach to Literature*
(1936), *Understanding Poetry* (1938), *Modern Rhetoric* (1949), and
American Literature: The Makers and the Making (1973). The principal
reason for his considerable literary reputation, of course, lies in his
dozen books of fiction and a similar number of books of poetry.

Victor H. Strandberg, the author of two books assessing Warren's
achievement as poet, suggests that Warren's poetic development can best
be understood and appreciated if his career is divided into three phases.
The first includes Warren's first three books—*Thirty-Six Poems* (1935),
Eleven Poems on the Same Theme (1942), and *Selected Poems* (1944)—
all of which demonstrate the influence of Warren's association with the
Fugitives. This phase culminates in "The Ballad of Billie Potts," a poem
which prefigures Warren's movement outside the Fugitive influence, at
least in matters of technique. Almost all of his early poetry is written in
the tightly disciplined style, the complex and densely textured manner,
that critics have come to associate with the high modern period—the age
best represented by the poetry of Eliot, Tate, and Pound. It is a poetry
filled with erudite, obscure, and esoteric allusions—one which is unified
not by structural obviousness but by imagistic relationships. Although
Warren moved away from the stylistic mannerisms of this formative
period, he never abandoned the basic concerns that make this poetry

uniquely his own. There is a compelling notion running through the earliest of these poems — with their repetition of such words as "withered," "frosty," "bloated," and "rotting," and their recurring images of decaying and putrifying vegetation — that man cannot escape the ever-present realization of his own mortality and his ultimate extinction. Near the end of the period the poet seems to find a more nearly acceptable solution to the problems related to the necessity of living in an imperfect world. Warren has indicated his almost obsessive interest in "the personal past and the past that lies behind that personal past — the problems that come to us as we contemplate the past in our world of mobility and disorientation." The general pattern of a Warren poem of this first period is about as follows: The young protagonist finds evil in the world he inhabits, so he attempts to escape through flight. He is seeking a "new innocence to be stayed by"; what he finds, however, is that he cannot return to his world of "the lost paradise." He must live in a world of time, sin, and death, one in which evil is always present. His only reconciliation to a loss of innocence and an introduction to a world of experience is a kind of self-irony, an acceptance of his fate, a kind of satisfaction in the realization he can never escape. Although the protagonist's awareness of his sense of loss is acute and despite his desperate need for an assurance of spiritual wholeness, the nearest he can come to any kind of inner satisfaction and contentment is the realization that only "in separateness does love learn definition."

In the poems of the middle period — from "The Ballad of Billie Potts," through *Brother to Dragons, Promises,* and *You, Emperors, and Others* — and those of the last period, all of those written since 1960, Warren has not deviated much from this general statement of the thematic concerns of his poetry. In an obvious attempt to reflect some of the complexities of the modern world, he has diversified his technique, his poetry is more personal in tone (though never quite dropping to the confessional level of some of Robert Lowell's poems), and he has demonstrated that grace is to be found in some of the most unlikely and unsuspected places. Not only does his recent poetry reveal more of his personal and private affections, but its deliberately rougher texture and structure clearly show the poet's attempt to capture the rhythms of common speech. Still some critics accuse him of thematic monotony; these readers find in his verse excessive morbidity, too much decay, terror, and disgust. Warren's view of man and nature and ultimate reality is too stark, unregenerative, and bleak for the more optimistic of his readers, but the consensus seems to be that he may be remembered as a poet who wrote novels. As Professor Harold Bloom of Yale University, an influential modern critic, writes, "He is the only living American poet of the stature of Frost and Stevens."

Of Warren's twelve novels, written between 1939 and 1977, the one most appreciated by both the critic and the general reader—in all editions approximately twenty-five million copies have been sold—is *All the King's Men* (1946). Not only is this the best political novel written in America in the twentieth century, it also delineates vividly and evocatively modern man succesfully confronting and controlling some of the most devastating problems of his time. Like the narrator in some of Warren's poems, Jack Burden, the protagonist of *All the King's Men,* first attempts to meet the problems of everyday living by trying to forget them in the hope they will go away ("The Big Sleep") or by attempting to escape from them through flight ("The Journey West"). Only when he discovers that neither of these devices will obliterate the imperfections from the world he must live in does he adopt the positivism and pragmatism of his age. He joins a political dictator, Willie Stark, who insists that one must judge ends not means. Man, a complicated piece of mechanism, is no more responsible for the results of his actions than the dead frog in the laboratory is for the twitch in the muscle in his leg when a charge of electricity is passed through it ("The Great Twitch"). Only after he has been responsible for Anne Stanton's giving herself to Willie Stark—Anne is the only girl Jack has ever loved—and he has observed his two best friends lying dead, is Jack able to put the details of his life into proper perspective, a feat he is able to accomplish by pondering deeply and seriously the actions of Cass Mastern, a maternal ancestor whose actions he has never been able to understand. He awakes one morning to discover that he no longer believes in "The Great Twitch." For the first time he understands why Cass Mastern, who unintentionally caused the death of his best friend and a slave girl named Phebe, deliberately gave up his own life. Jack Burden moves into the final stage of his philosophical development ("The Spider Web"):

> Cass Mastern lived for a few years and in that time he learned that the world is all of one piece. He learned that the world is like an enormous spider web, and if you touch it, however lightly, at any point, the vibration ripples to the remotest perimeter and the drowsy spider feels the tingle. . . . It does not matter whether or not you meant to brush the web of things.

Jack learns that not only must he accept full responsibility for his actions, but he must also assume responsibility for any repercussions of the initial act. Only in this way can men live as human beings in a world that seems to have lost its direction, its aims, its sense of purpose.

At a time when man is looking to science and social science for answers to questions that those disciplines cannot provide, John Crowe Ransom realized that modern man was neglecting, through his own ignorance, one of the sources from which he could get the information he needed so desperately. That source was poetry, through which man is able to know the concrete particularities of the world in which he lives. Because of the emphasis of certain poets of the nineteenth century and the interpretations of some of their readers, poetry had come to be regarded, Ransom felt, as a means of *idealizing* the world and as a series of didactic or moralizing statements (ideas), decorated with as many pleasing pictures (images) as the poet felt were necessary to illustrate adequately his ideas. In dozens of essays and three books, Ransom attempted to destroy this fallacious view of poetry and to provide an accurate account of the nature and function of the poetic discourse because, as he expressed it, "no civilization has ever existed without poetry and we should not expect ours to be an exception." Ransom's imaginative writing on aesthetics, particularly poetry, established him as one of the few genuinely theoretical critics this country has produced.

Ransom's theories were expanded and made more utilitarian through the critical writing of one of his former students, Allen Tate. In fact Ransom has admitted that a free exchange of ideas with Tate, through conversations and letters, was of fundamental assistance to him in developing his critical principles. Two other students of Ransom's, Robert Penn Warren and Cleanth Brooks, took Ransom's and Tate's theories of the cognitive function of literature, theories that insist that poetry can provide a kind of knowledge that modern man needs and can get almost nowhere else. Brooks and Warren reshaped and expressed these theories in their own language and passed them on to the general public. In a series of innovative textbooks, the most influential of which was *Understanding Poetry,* they made this new "approach" to literary art available to students in the colleges and secondary schools. They demonstrated how literature must be read if it is to reveal the unique knowledge it contains, and they expressed convincingly the importance of one attempting to acquire this kind of knowledge.

The literary scene in Tennessee in the late thirties and early forties was not completely dominated by the statement and dissemination of Ransom's significant theories of the nature and function of poetry. During these years Allen Tate and Cleanth Brooks wrote important critical es-

says of their own, and by the beginning of World War II, Robert Penn
Warren had established his reputation as one of the most original, enduring, and versatile literary figures in American history. The poems,
essays, and novels he wrote between 1935 and 1944 have earned him an
international reputation, and they emphasize in their evocative and convincing presentation of the plight of modern man, the value of the literary theories discussed in this chapter as few other creations could.

5. The Contemporary Scene

Although, as many commentators have pointed out, the South appears to have lost, sometime after World War II, the honor of being the literary capital of the United States, there seems to have been no noticeable decrease in either the quantity or the quality of literary productivity in Tennessee in the past thirty-five years or so. Of the dozens of promising young writers — and others with more established careers — space will permit the detailed consideration of only four whose best work has been done, or has become available, since the close of World War II: Mildred Haun, James Agee, Peter Taylor, and Cormac McCarthy.

Mildren Haun (1911–66) was born in Hamblen County but grew up in Haun Hollow in the Hoot Owl District of Cocke County, the area in which almost all of her unique and strangely evocative and convincing stories are set. For sixteen years she lived in this region rich in folkways and folktales, before going to Franklin, Tennessee, to live with relatives so that she could attend a modern secondary school. Her motivation for finishing high school, an accomplishment rarely achieved in Haun Hollow, was to prepare her to enter Vanderbilt University, where she earned a B.A. degree (1935) and an M.A. (1937). Above all else, she wanted to attend medical school to prepare herself to be a modern "granny-woman," one who traditionally attended to the needs of the sick, served as a mid-wife when a child was born, and "laid-out" the dead.

Her introduction to calculus and to some of the advanced science courses required for admission to the Vanderbilt Medical School convinced her that she must change her career objective; consequently, with the encouragement of John Crowe Ransom and Donald Davidson, she took additional English courses and decided to complete a major in that area. At the same time, in Ransom's advanced composition course, she began to write seriously, presenting a literal deluge of stories based on the rich, varied, and unusual experiences of her Cocke County child-

hood. She became so deeply immersed in the stories, songs, legends, folkways, and superstitions of her native region that she decided to remain at Vanderbilt and complete the requirements for a master's degree in English, which she received in June 1937. Her master's thesis, done under the direction of Donald Davidson, was entitled "Cocke County Ballads and Songs," one of the most valuable collections of southern folk songs ever compiled. Her work with Davidson on this important collection made Miss Haun more fully aware of her East Tennessee heritage, and this awareness influenced every story she ever wrote.

After her graduation from Vanderbilt, she studied briefly at the State University of Iowa, before bringing out, in 1941, *The Hawk's Done Gone,* the only collection of her stories published in her lifetime. This collection quickly went out of print, and although Miss Haun continued to write for the remainder of her life, only one story of hers was published after 1941, until the Vanderbilt University Press brought out *The Hawk's Done Gone and Other Stories* (1968), which contains ten stories not previously collected. Mildred Haun's literary reputation, which is based on this collection, is far beneath that merited by the originality, the technical dexterity, the undeniable force of these unusual tales of witchcraft, incest, miscegenation, and infanticide. Despite their strange and almost unbelievable plots, made plausible and convincing only by the use of a reliable and persuasive narrator, the stories keep the reader, despite his cynical scientific orientation, under their spell because their author creates in the first paragraph and maintains to the last sentence an illusion of reality. Given these particular characters and this strangely unique appearing set of circumstances, it is difficult to imagine the story developing in any way except that in which it does, seeming to evolve as naturally and unpredictably as a summer's day, which opens with a clear and brilliant sunrise and moves through a turbulent, destructive, and unexpected thunderstorm before ending in a peaceful, breathtakingly beautiful sunset. One experiences a Haun story as one lives through such a day in the deep South, not only unaware of the beauty and splendor of his natural surroundings, but strangely stirred and rendered vaguely uneasy by the suggestion of an undeniable relationship between these natural forces and a supernatural realm lying just beyond that bounded by sensory perception and rational apprehension.

Above: A scene in Cocke County, 1930s. *Below:* Mildred Haun about 1935. *Photographs from Jesse E. Wills Collection.*

A unique area of human experience is delineated by Mary Darthula White Kanipe, Miss Haun's *persona*. She is the mother of an illegitimate son and married to a man with no apparent affection for her nor any compassion for his neighbor. He is the father, by a previous marriage, of a group of subhuman sons; Mrs. Kanipe has been "Granny-woman" of three generations of children of her community and the most widely respected person in the entire county. The stories she relates include the horrible, the selfish, the fantastic, the ignorant, the brutal, the overtly superstitious, and the harsh, ever demanding reality of living in a backward, remote community. They embrace, too, the tenderness of mother love, the protective regard of parent-for-child and child-for-parent; the rewards of living in a clearly defined, closely-knit community with its well-understood rites, rituals, and ceremonies; the unquestioned merits of man's attempting to establish a right relation to his community, to nature, and to God. The material of these stories mixes without clearly marked distinctions the natural and supernatural. Whatever the subject the diction never varies. It is always vivid, sharp, and concrete, decorated with functional, homely figures of speech taken directly from likenesses in the natural world. Most importantly, as far as its effectiveness as a means of exact, memorable communication is concerned, is the fact that it is always delivered by a compelling, believable, convincing mountain woman, whom Miss Haun allows to describe herself in the Prologue to *The Hawk's Done Gone* and then leaves her to tell the stories, without authorial intrusion: "I've been Granny-woman to every youngon born in this district for nigh sixty years now. I've tied the navel cords of all the saints and sinners that have seen their first daylight in Hoot Owl District. They all have bellies about alike. There's not much difference." Considered together, Miss Haun's stories present a combination of human attitudes, relationships, and experiences that can be found in few other sources. This distinctively identifying quality of her writing is admirably summarized in Professor Herschel Gower's illuminating introduction to his edition of *The Hawk's Done Gone and Other Stories:*

> Consciously or unconsciously, few writers in the twentieth century have set down as complex a rendering of romantic fantasy and realism. Perhaps few have had as informed a "folk" background or been as willing to take as many chances with their readers. The thematic premise, bluntly put, insists upon equal parts of witchcraft and herb medicine. The memorable narrator is simultaneously a witch-doctor and mountain midwife. Thus the final integrity of these disparate elements makes for strong purgation. Because the stories are always

within hearing distance of the folk tradition, they provide us with a link between the ancient oral tale and its full-grown modern descendants. To read them is to confront again those same powers operative and prevailing in epic and myth; they are the passionate, supernatural forces which are at work simultaneously in Miss Haun's corner of the universe and in Homer's.

Although the geographic area Miss Haun is writing about is near that in which Mary Noailles Murfree's stories are set, and the patterns of speech are almost the same, there the similarity ends. Miss Haun's characters are not idealized, virtuous noble savages untouched by the evils of civilization. Instead there are distinct and broad gradations of morality among them — the almost perfect and the nearly imperfect, the wise and the stupid, the cruel and the compassionate, the beastly and the angelic. Some of the stories delineate situations too horrible to contemplate if they were told by anyone except a sensible, tolerant, sympathetic narrator. "The Pit of Death" concerns a series of cruel hoaxes thrust upon Joe White, the narrator's illegitimate son, by his acquaintances. No one, except Tiny Brock, will accept Joe because of his unknown father and the color of his skin. (Joe is a Melungeon, a frontier people probably descended from a mixture of whites, Indians, and free blacks.) The girls at school make fun of Tiny's apron because it is made of homespun cloth, yelling at her at recess time that no one will "spark Tiny but a bastard" and calling her "a lost dog in love with a bastard." Joe and Tiny become "dern sweethearts," nevertheless, and spend all of their free time together, playing childhood games, walking in the woods, or fishing and hunting. As Joe grows older, he begins to trap; he becomes so successful catching game when no one else can, that many men ask where he traps, but he will never tell. Some suspect him of setting traps in a cave between his home and the Brockes': "A few folks thought Joe knowed some paths through that cave between Brock's house and here. They allowed there were all sorts of animals in there but nobody had ever been able to get further back into it than five or six yards. They allowed Joe might have found a path through it or maybe some other opening. I don't know. He did sometimes grin mighty big when he heard folks talk about that cave going straight down instead of back into Reds Run Mountain like other caves."

Finally Tiny's father forbids her to marry Joe; he will not even allow them to see each other, and they begin meeting in the woods. Soon Tiny becomes pregnant, and just before she is to deliver, Joe says he is going to bring her to his mother so she can take care of her. Immediately after

Joe leaves for her, Ad, his step-father, follows him with his gun. About midnight Ad returns and his wife notices that he "looked sneaking— more sneaking than a sheep-killing dog." Nine days later Tiny has her baby and Mary, in her capacity as "Granny-woman," is called to assist. She dreads having to walk alone in front of the cave when she returns home early on the following morning: "I feared to pass that cave. When I got close to it, I felt like wooly bugs were crawling all over me. It was so quiet I could have heard a feather drop. I tried to run past. My legs wouldn't work. Something made me stop—right in front of the cave. Chains rattling in it. Animals hollering. And a man's voice—Joe's voice. I knowed it was his voice. And I was sure."

Many of the stories concern witchcraft or incest, and one or two of the most compelling combine these two motifs. In "Barshia's Horse He Made, It Flew," Barshia Kanipe, Ad's son by his first wife, has perpetual motion in his right leg, and Mary finds this peculiarity downright irritating: "Having him forever patting the floor was enough to run a hog wild. And just seeing him setting there with his legs all sprawled out. All sprawled out and one foot a-going up and down pickety peck—no matter what a body was trying to do." Then she began to notice that when Teelie Edes, a neighbor suspected of being a witch, comes to visit, she is absolutely fascinated by the movement of Barshia's foot: "She watched his foot like a hawk. Her head would go up and down to keep time with it. And her eyes would sparkle like a toad's eyes. . . . How her eyes looked, you know, that witchy stare." Mary always believed Teelie had marked Barshia with a witch's mark, but she could never be sure, although Dona Fawver, another neighbor, had told her that she had seen "Teelie pull off her dress one time and there was a brown spot on her left breast in the shape of a frog . . . a sure witch sign." Teelie has put the sign on Barshia, according to Dona, because "Teelie got mad at Barshia that day she told him not to kill that toad frog and he went on and did it anyhow." One of the principal reasons Mary wants to continue living is that she knows she will be called to "lay-out" Teelie when she dies and she wants "to see if she has got any witch marks on her."

Many of the stories develop around an incestuous relation, one of the most memorable of which is in "The New Jerusalem." Effena Kanipe marries Murf Owens, a Melungeon, and seems unnaturally concerned about allowing him to share her bridal bed, although she obviously loves him very much. Thinking her reluctance is natural virginal shyness, the women prepare her for the ritualistic event: "The womenfolks pulled off her last piece of clothes. She stood there limp as a hot cabbage leaf and let them put the gown on her. It was the first gown Effena had ever had. She made it herself. With a pink and white tatted yoke in it. Pink ribbon run through the tatting. . . . Dona Fawver raised Effena's arms up, and somebody else slipped the gown over her head. All together they lifted her up and laid her over on the far side of the bed — on the side next to the wall."

Then, amid much giggling, they ring the cowbell, announcing the newly wedded woman is ready to receive her husband. When Murf comes into the room, however, Effena clings to her side of the bed with her face to the wall. After Murf has blown out the light, she makes him light it again; then she turns to him and makes the one confession a woman of that time cannot make to her husband, "Murf, I'm not pyore." Even as devastating as this confession is, the truth that finally emerges is even worse. Effena is not "pyore" because she has been sexually assaulted by her half-brother Linus. Murf graciously forgives her because he knows she has not willingly submitted to Linus, but Linus, reluctant to give her up, murders Murf. Even though she is going to have her husband's child, Linus continues to take her against her will.

As can be concluded from the previous discussion, woman's lot in the region Miss Haun is writing about is not an easy one. In the title story, "The Hawk's Done Gone," the narrator stands helplessly by, while her husband and his son Linus dispose of her priceless heirlooms to an antique collector: the hand-made cherry bed in which she and all of her children, except Joe, were conceived and born; the spinning wheel and warping bars on which she had made the family's clothing; the green and gold bag that belonged to her mother (the one from which her lover Charles, Joe's father, had drunk); the trundle bed on which she and all of her children had slept, the one on which she had lain with Charles. Then Ad and Linus cut logs and trade them for thin, soft lumber to replace her sturdy log house that has stood unaffected by the passing of time for more than a hundred years. All of these things are invaluable to her, and their being senselessly disposed of for the pittance Ad and Linus are getting for them almost destroys her. Her whole life is shattering around her, and she is powerless to prevent it because the man she has been married to for forty years is as incapable of knowing the true value of the objects he is disposing of as he is of realizing the worth of his life-long companion. They and she are his to use as he will.

The two motifs, incest and witchcraft, are combined in "The Look," Miss Haun's most gruesomely frightening story, one not published until after her death. A large part of the effect of the story comes from the manner in which it is told. The point of view is that of a young woman, the only female child in a very large family. In a calm, matter-of-fact tone, she relates the inhumane manner in which she had been treated by her mother and two of her three surviving brothers, the others having died of "quick-going consumption." The story as it slowly develops offers a rational explanation of a rather cryptic opening statement: "She didn't say e'er a word as she was dying. Ma didn't. She just looked at me, like a cat looking at a bird, setting its eye on it, making it set still where it is. And I come back home. I couldn't a-handily been blamed if I hadn't, I reckon, if I had stayed away and let the boys shift for theirselves. But after that look that last morning I could do nothing else but come."

Only after we have read through the story are we aware of why she would not have been "blamed" if she had "let the boys shift for theirselves." After years in which she had been subjected to every indignity imaginable, she is living with a widowed cousin, who loves her, and for the first time in her life she is being treated like a human being. Her years at home have been filled with the most flagrant violations of her person conceivable: her two brothers have taken from her and sold property willed to her by her grandmother — cows, turkeys, chickens, and even her home. They have allowed the house to fall down around her; they have made her do outside work and have taken her wages from her; they have given her bed to their prostitute friends; they have beaten her repeatedly, often seeking release from frustrations arising from other sources; and one brother has sexually assaulted her since she was twelve. It is no wonder, then, that she felt no obligation to give up her comfortable situation to care for her brothers.

She does so only because of that *look* her dying mother gave her, and the significance of that *look* is the key to the story. Everytime she is mistreated by one of her brothers, the mother always defends the brothers, and the narrator thinks for a long time her mother's treatment of her is the result of her being "unwanted" by her father and by her mother's liking for boys. She said "she didn't want a girl youngon," the narrator reveals: "I reckon she meant it." Why "she meant it," we learn near the end of the story. From a conversation with her cousin, the narrator learns that a "witch woman" loses "their power with men folks when a girl youngon is born to them." Her mother resented her coming because, being a witch, she lost her power over men. Also the apparently innocent look of a dying mother beseeching her daughter to look after her brothers is really a witch's stare placing the victim under her spell. The girl gives up her place of security for the same reason she has accepted her brothers' mistreatment through the years. She is bewitched (or thinks she is) and has no will of her own.

This story demonstrates the curious blend of "romantic fantasy" and "realism" that forms some of Miss Haun's most gripping narratives, and it reveals, too, how far Miss Haun is willing to push the reader's credulity. In fact in almost all of her stories the boundaries separating fact from fantasy are dimly marked and the distance between the physical and metaphysical world, never very great, is remarkably easy to traverse. The world of nature, always close at hand, offers unlimited means of foretelling the future—of knowing God's plan for man, or of recognizing the intervention of the devil in the affairs of the world—if man only knows how to read the signs: when a witch dies her cow gives bloody milk; the use of silver bullets are the only means of killing witches; the only way a man can neutralize the spell of a witch is by standing in water up to his knees. One can identify a witch by placing a broom across a doorway because a witch cannot step across a broom. The cry of an owl foretells death. Burning sassafras roots always results in a tragedy in the family. One character in a story talks to God through a bluebird. In several stories spirits of the recently dead return to protect their loved ones or to prevent them from doing foolish things. Marriages consummated while red haw bushes are in bloom will always end in tragedy. A dove singing on a house top means death within a year. One character speaks to her mother in heaven and learns it takes ninety-one days for the spirit of one recently dead to move from earth to heaven. As Professor Gower has observed, "the stories are always within hearing distance of the folk tradition," and they provide an important "link between the ancient oral tale and its full-grown moral descendants."

Few writers could be further removed from each other, both in the subject matter about which they wrote and in the manner in which they presented their material, than were Mildred Haun and James Agee. The setting of Haun's stories is rural and isolated; they are given credibility by a first-person narrator who seldom goes beyond the surface details of the strange narrative she is relating. Agee's novels have urban settings; he often presents a character's thoughts and feelings through an omniscient narrator. This technique is used because often the basic action of the narrative is within a character, involving basic psychological change in feeling or attitude toward someone or something. Despite these obvious differences, however, the geographical locations in which their narratives occur are only a few miles apart, and the actions of many of them are separated by less than fifty years.

James Agee (1909–55) is usually characterized as an extraordinarily gifted man who never achieved the artistic stature he should have because of his inability to focus his talent on any one literary genre. In a comparatively brief life, much of which he had to devote to journalism in order to earn a living, he produced a book of verse, *Permit Me Voyage* (1934), *Let Us Now Praise Famous Men* (1941), and a novella, *The Morning Watch* (1951). He also served as a book reviewer for *Time,* as a film critic for both *Time* and *Nation,* and as a full-time feature writer for *Fortune.* He wrote many movie scripts, including one based on some of Stephen Crane's stories, and his most memorable scripts were *The African Queen* and *The Night of the Hunter.* In 1957, two years after his death, *A Death in the Family,* a very uneven novel detailing many of Agee's life-long attitudes and concerns, was published. This novel won the Pulitzer Prize in 1960.

Born in Knoxville, Tennessee, Agee was educated at St. Andrews (1916–24) in Sewanee, Tennessee, at the public schools of Knoxville (1924–25), at Phillips Exeter Academy (1925–28), and at Harvard (1928–32). At Harvard, where he spent much of his time writing poetry and contributing to the literary magazine, he attracted the attention of Dwight McDonald, who assisted him in getting a position at *Fortune* magazine. Shortly after beginning work for *Fortune,* the Yale Younger Poets Series brought out Agee's only book of poetry, *Permit Me Voyage,* much of which had been written while he was in college. A very private and personal book, closely related to, but not as frank and open as those books of verse later labeled as "confessional poetry," the poems in this volume are lyrical expressions of Agee's basic concerns: his most private and carefully guarded thoughts on love, the awareness of his own mortality, and his antithetical attitudes on the existence of a God concerned about the affairs of man. Soon after the book was published, Agee wrote Father James Harold Flye, who was a member of the faculty of St. Andrews while Agee was a student there and who remained his friend for the rest of Agee's brief life, that he felt now that the formal demands of traditional verse were too restrictive to allow poetry to be a means of significant literary expression. For the remainder of his life Agee discussed his most intimate personal problems and his literary aspirations and disappointments with Father Flye.

James Agee shortly after his graduation from Harvard. *Photograph used by permission of St. Andrew's School.*

At *Fortune,* Agee focused all his talent on the mundane journalistic assignments that he and his researcher received. As a result, he quickly raised the quality of some of the feature stories that magazine carried to a level never again achieved by a publication of that sort in America. In 1936 *Fortune* commissioned Agee and Walker Evans, a photographer borrowed from the Farm Security Administration, to go to Alabama to do an interpretative article on the plight of the tenant farmer. With the Great Depression affecting the economic health of the entire nation and the readers' sympathy for the underdog aroused by the fiction of writers like Erskine Caldwell and John Steinbeck and hundreds of journalists from the most influential journals in America, such an essay seemed a natural, particularly when it came from the pen of a journalist with the demonstrated expertise of the most effective writer on the *Fortune* staff. In Alabama, however, Agee's interest in the assignment changed, and in large measure that of Evans did too; consequently they stayed much longer than their editors intended. When they returned, therefore, they brought back many more photographs than the magazine could use and a written text that did not accomplish at all what the magazine expected. The intent of Evans's photographs and Agee's essay was not to make some emotionally wrought comment upon the miserable plight of the tenant farmer but to present faithfully the impact of the fact of share-cropping on the human sensibility. The essay did not contain, therefore, a logically organized, chronologically developed argument. Many editorial conferences were devoted to the subject, but *Fortune* finally decided it could not use the pictures or the essay. After five years of polishing their material and securing permission to publish it elsewhere, Agee and Evans presented it to Houghton, Mifflin, who brought it out as *Let Us Now Praise Famous Men.* Although some authorities state that only six hundred of the original run of one thousand copies were sold, it is a work of high art, unlike anything else ever done in America, and many consider it Agee's most important artistic accomplishment.

In *The Morning Watch,* as the anonymous reviewer in *Time* pointed out, "James Agee has come close to a small triumph; he has pierced the protective shell of a boy's personality and exposed the religious exaltations of the boy without once falling into bathos." During the morning watch on Good Friday, the twelve-year-old Richard cannot keep his attention centered completely on his devotions because he is aware of the pressure of his knees on the rough altar rail, and of the strain on his back because of the prolonged kneeling. He is horrified, as the reader is, when he recalls his eating worms as a means of self-mortification. Trying to identify with a sacrificial Christ, he can only imagine himself nailed to the cross, where he hangs stoically and uncomplainingly, and the best athlete in school whispering, "Jesus, that kid has guts!" His every thought, he feels, is tainted with pride and he can only pray, "O God forgive me if you can stand to." Agee's great achievement, it would seem, is in making us aware of Richard's fervent attempts to accept an all-abiding faith amid his own inadequacies and his classmates' conduct that borders on obscene grossness. Despite the seriousness of the theme and the sincerity of Richard's search, the tone of the book is neither heavy nor depressing. Above all, Agee does not lapse into sentimentality or didacticism. Within the rather strict limits he set for himself — he does not intrude upon the boy's reactions nor does he attempt to refine or to comment upon Richard's interpretation of the significance of a specific experience—Agee's achievement is considerable. After reading this book, most critics labeled Agee "a novelist of promise," and they anxiously awaited the appearance of his next work of fiction.

Agee's next novel was not published until 1957, two years after his death from a sudden heart attack. For several years he had been working on two manuscripts. One was to be a large rambling account, much in the manner of Thomas Wolfe, of the controversies and resentments arising from the marriage of two members of large, drastically different families. The other was to be a tightly unified textual evocation of his early childhood, the traumatic experience of which was the death of his father when he was very young. This treatment was to deal with the effects of the death of Jay Follett upon his six-year-old son, Rufus. The book that Agee's editors put together, as Leslie Fiedler, the noted American critic, has pointed out, is obviously composed of some of both of these manuscripts. (Fiedler's theory has been widely accepted because of his critical reputation, based primarily on *Love and Death in the American Novel*.) The threat of drunkenness and the clash between the two families of in-laws, both only sketchily developed, come from the proposed long manuscript on which Agee had not passed far beyond the planning and outlining stage. The two other thematic concerns — the terrible reality of death and the inevitable clash between Protestantism and Catholicism — come from the much briefer and more nearly completed manuscript, and the attempt to combine the two narratives, so vastly different in both conception and execution, results in a confused, because never identified, point of view. Even the chapters devoted to Rufus's growing awareness of his father's presence — and he becomes truly aware of his father's existence only when his consciousness is completely occupied by the empty space created by his father's absence—are not limited to Rufus's sensibility, although the post of observation is just beyond his head. Other sections are strongly focused on the mother's thoughts and feelings, and the opening chapter employs a cinematic technique, scanning an entire city, Knoxville, Tennessee, on a late summer afternoon in 1915. As the camera moves, it focuses briefly on the houses, the streets, and the trees, fences, and hedges; the sounds as well as sights are recorded by the sweeping camera; therefore the reader hears the locusts and the frogs, the yelling of the children playing in the streets, and the soft murmur of the voices of adults sitting on the front porches or hovering around barbecue grills in the backyards. (Agee never identifies the section of Knoxville he is describing, but he writes that it is a "lower, middle class" district, "the houses are middle-sized" and constructed in the late nineteenth century.) From this section one gets an impression of the unique flavor of growing up in a middle-sized southern city in the first decades of this century. A chapter about midway through the book, detailing an afternoon's visit by the Folger family to the home of their one-hundred-and-three-year-old grandmother, is told by an omniscient narrator. Both the prelude and this chapter evidently come from the longer, unformed fragment. Professor Fiedler indicates precisely the moving and lasting effect that the book has on most readers: "[I]t would be ungrateful and unforgiveable not to say what *pleasure* there is in his visual revelations. The sights (and though primarily these, beyond them, the smells, tastes, textures, sounds) of Knoxville, Tennessee, some forty years ago, are rendered with an astonishing tact and precision, with a kind of freshness that belongs, for most of us, only to the memories of childhood. It is in the lyrical, free, sensual evocation of a boy's world . . . of experience upon which others depend and from which they hopelessly decline that Agee excells."

The intricacy with which Agee renders with unquestioned fidelity his characters' sensory impressions and the disturbing movements of their thoughts, feelings, and impressions can become tedious. For example, for almost two pages we hear the sounds made by the engine of Jay's car as he tries to start it on the last day of his life. Agee's insatiable desire for realism does not succeed in this case. His detailed description of how a sluggish motor sounds when one is trying to get it started on a cold morning is precise and exact, but this passage does not function as it should. At best it is a *tour de force* because the reader is interested in Mary's (the mother's) feelings, and the prolonged attention to the sound of the grinding motor is a distraction. Readers could have shared Mary's feelings, as she waits for her husband to leave on a journey that for some inexplicable reason she knows is to be his last. If Agee had concentrated on attempting to evoke precisely *what* and *how* she feels at this moment, he could have retained the reader's undivided attention. Instead, Agee offers a two-page onomatopoeic description of the sound of a balky motor getting underway and diverts his reader from the story he is telling.

Some of Agee's efforts to recreate the "sensual evocation" of a six-year-old boy are much more successful. Early in the novel, Rufus and his father are returning from a movie when they approach a corner where his father often stops to relax for a moment before going on home:

> Rufus had come recently to feel a quiet kind of anticipation of the corner, from the moment they finished crossing the viaduct; and, during the ten to twenty minutes they sat on the rock, a particular kind of contentment, unlike any other that he knew. He did not know what this was, in words or ideas, or what the reason was; it was simply all he saw and felt. It was, mainly, knowing that his father, too, felt a particular kind of contentment, here, unlike any other, and that their kinds of contentment were much alike, and depended on each other. Rufus seldom had at all sharply the feeling that he and his father were estranged, yet they must have been, and he must have felt it, for always during these quiet moments on the rock a part of his sense of complete contentment lay in the feeling that they were reconciled. . . . He felt that although his father loved their home and loved all of them, he was more lonely than the contentment of this family love could help; that it even increased his loneliness, or made it hard for him not to be lonely. He felt that sitting out here, he was not lonely; or if he was, that he felt on good terms with the loneliness; that he was a homesick man, and that here on the rock, though he might be more homesick than ever, he was well. He knew that a very important part of his well-being came of staying a few minutes away from home, very quietly, in the dark, listening to the leaves if they moved, and looking at the stars; and that his own, Rufus' own presence, was fully as indispensable to this well-being. . . . These realizations moved clearly through the senses, the memory the feelings, the mere feeling of the place they paused at, about a quarter of a mile from home, on a rock under a stray tree that had grown in the city, their feet on undomesticated clay, facing north through the night over the Southern Railway tracks and over North Knoxville, toward the deeply folded small mountains and the Powell River Valley, and above them, the trembling lanterns of the universe, seeming so near, so intimate, that when air stirred the leaves and their hair, it seemed to be the breathing, the whispering of the stars.

In the passage from which this long quotation was taken—and it covers at least six pages—Agee succeeds in reconstituting the intensity and quality of the feelings of a six-year-old boy and his *sense* of his father's feelings. Writing of this kind, so eloquent yet so precise and functional, appears only in the work of a writer like Faulkner, Joyce, or Proust. At the top of his form, Agee's prose—in a *Fortune* article, in a movie review, or in *Let Us Now Praise Famous Men*—was a finely tuned instrument of which he was in complete control. There were few textures of meaning or nuances of feeling he could not recreate.

Despite its obvious weaknesses, *Death in the Family* demonstrates that Agee had "all the equipment of a considerable novelist, and of a very original one from the angle of a technique." It is not only an original book, but one that demonstrates—as does nothing else Agee wrote, except *Let Us Now Praise Famous Men*—how effective the English language is in the hands of a master. Always willing to reduce the narrative significance of his novel to the dramatically lyrical, Agee is able to make the reader know the reality and the devastating force of human grief as few other writers ever have. No one has contributed more to our ability to comprehend the awesome reality of death.

One of the most accomplished short story writers of the twentieth century, Peter Taylor, in his careful attentions to the technical details of his craft, is reminiscent of Agee. But there the similarity ends, for much of Taylor's fiction is concerned with the changes that have occurred in the quality of life available in a society that is rapidly shifting from agrarian to urban in orientation. He was born into a well-to-do, firmly established family in Trenton, Tennessee, on January 8, 1917. The son of a successful lawyer, state attorney general, and insurance executive, his background included not only financial security and social respectability, but his was a family of obvious political prominence, having furnished two state governors—Alfred A. Taylor and Robert L. Taylor—a federal judge and many other less significant public officials. Taylor's stories are set in the places in which he lived and knew well—Trenton, Nashville, St. Louis, and Memphis. His determination to become a writer, an ambition he harbored from early adolescence, was strengthened by the persons under whom he studied. At Southwestern-at-Memphis he was a student of Allen Tate's. Later he transferred to Vanderbilt because John Crowe Ransom was there, and, in 1938, followed Ransom to Kenyon, from which he was graduated in 1940. He enrolled in Louisiana State University in 1940 because Cleanth Brooks and Robert Penn Warren were on the faculty there, but Taylor soon withdrew in order to have more time to write. A careful, cautious writer, over the past thirty years he has published six collections of short stories, a novel, and three dramas.

The protagonist of the Taylor story is usually a resident of a middle-sized city of the upper South, although he is more often than not one or two generations removed from a small Southern town, usually the fictitious Thornton, Tennessee. These quiet tales of domestic life almost always reveal — just beneath the level of the slightly perturbed world of families, businesses, servants, and matter-of-factness on which the principal action occurs — a sense of deep tragedy, disorder, and often impending doom. Many of these tales are leisurely told by a narrator who is urbane, witty, sophisticated, nostalgic — very much like Taylor himself — a gentleman who is confiding in a lady or another gentleman, someone who shares the creature comforts of those who belong to the financially secure, and often wealthy, world of the upper-middle class: doctors, lawyers, businessmen, judges, college presidents, and even governors. Theirs is a society securely rooted in tradition and history, but the courteous, patient confidante in his matter-of-fact, understated manner often reveals to his listeners an unsuspected characteristic of this placid, most natural of all possible worlds. What he presents is something that is always significant, usually much broader in application than the precisely delineated world in which it occurs, and nearly always unsettling and disturbing — sometimes so shocking and horrible that the narrator's auditor is filled with disgust or terror. Stories such as "Venus, Cupid, Folly, and Time" describe spiritual incest and suggest the possibility of physical incest as well. "A Spinster's Tale," narrated by a young girl, reveals the distorted, grotesque horrors of a warped, neurotic imagination. "The Fancy Woman" presents a sordid, illicit affair between a hard drinking, good-time girl and a brutish, egocentric, pleasure-seeking but unfeeling member of the so-called respectable wealthy class. Although no reference is made specifically by either of the principal characters in the story, the Negro maid in "Cookie" exposes the emptiness, the meaninglessness of the marriage between a successful, middle-aged doctor and his wife. After the maid has revealed that it is a well-known fact around town that the doctor is meeting "the ladies" at the home of a friend of his, and after he has left for another assignation, the wife first thinks she will fire Cookie because she cannot have "a servant of mine talking to my husband like that." After thinking the matter over — although she will never admit what the reader surely knows — she tells her husband, "I'll speak to her tonight. It'll never happen again." She is caught in a loveless union from which she can never escape and can only think, pathetically, perhaps it will not be true; or in some way the pain will be easier to bear, if she does not admit the glaringly evident truth, even to herself.

The world of Peter Taylor's stories includes the inevitable nostalgia and feeling of separation that accompanies one's leaving his hometown, the nagging ever-present realization that one can never recapture the feelings, the aspirations, and the experiences of his youth. The constant awareness of his own mortality, of his movement from innocence through experience to death, is like a cancer forever growing larger within him. (The best of these stories is "At the Drug Store.") That world includes, too, an ambiguous view of the family: not only a unifying, civilizing institution but one that is simultaneously stultifying, imprisoning, and destructive of one's individual development. ("In the Miro District," one of his most recent stories, delineates poignantly and compellingly the unhappy results of a family's accepting the stereotype that a grand-father and his grandson should be buddies. The individual personalities and differences will not permit this kind of relationship between persons of different generations.) Taylor's segment of the world that he knows so well embraces, too, a disintegrating tradition, the deterioration of family, the tensions of love—of family, of home, of parents, of childhood sweethearts—and the loneliness that always follows the realization that one is cut off from tradition and family; that in the modern materialistic world, with its hurry, efficiency, and constant anxieties, free, open honest communication is virtually impossible. This is the world which, Robert Penn Warren says, Taylor "has made his own forever." As one critic has pointed out, "Peter Taylor is our southern Chekov, as Faulkner was our Dostoevsky"; the violence forever lying just beneath the seemingly peaceful exterior is always boiling and threatening to explode.

Taylor's well-crafted stories of the gentlefolk of the upper South are not propaganda pieces. He is attempting, as good artists always are, to reconstitute reality, not to make some comment about a particular social order. His stories, as Robert K. Morris, a reviewer for *The Nation,* has observed, reveal to us a "particular kind of sensibility: a sensibility encased in memories that have saddened or weakened it without having to-

---

Above: Peter Taylor in 1972. *Jesse E. Wills Collection. Below:* Cormac McCarthy about 1973. *Random House.*

tally destroyed or done violence to it." Few authors in modern southern literature equal Taylor in his ability to ferret out the secret motives that move his people to act precisely as they do:

> Taylor's characters are flesh and blood, not beautiful losers but well-groomed, civilized plain ones who have, for one reason or another, lost something of themselves somewhere along the way. Nostalgia, failure, loneliness, the pains of growing up, the inability to communicate or respond, the gulf between people — these are his themes. There is scarcely a story . . . which is not undercut with irony, even in the intensest moments of its poignancy and pathos; scarcely one in which outwardly simple surfaces do not dissolve into underlying psychological complexities; or one in which an encounter, a familiar occurrence, an all too human gesture does not bring insight or awareness.

Although for almost thirty years Taylor's stories have retained their sure and certain grasp of the unique quality of Tennessee mores and manners, his attitude toward this territory, which he has staked out as his exclusive property, has not changed a great deal. This amazingly consistent view of reality is dramatically revealed, most readers believe, in one of his early stories, the title story in his first collection.

The focus of this early narrative, "The Long Fourth," is upon Harriet Wilson, a Nashville housewife approaching middle-age, who is preparing for a visit home from her son, a journalist living in New York. He is coming for a long weekend before being inducted into the army during World War II. Harriet has induced all members of her family and household staff — her husband, her two daughters, her cook, Mattie, and Mattie's nephew, B.T., a general handyman around the place — to assist her in making this visit one that Son will long remember. She has planned a party, a family friend is to entertain them with a dinner party, and there are scheduled periods for family togetherness.

Despite her attention to every possible detail, all does not work out as expected, and a consideration of all of these insignificant details that will not fit into her preconceived mold reveals how chaotic and traditionless her seemingly placid and ordered life really is. First of all Mattie comes to Harriet, prostrate with grief, to reveal that B.T. is leaving after the weekend to work in a defense plant. Although Harriet is secretly pleased that B.T. is leaving, she cannot reveal her true feeling to Mattie. ("He had neither the good manners nor the affectionate nature nor the appealing humor that niggers often have." Every weekend he brings wenches to his cabin in the backyard where they drink, fight, carouse, and fornicate for two or three days. Worst of all, B.T. has nauseating body odor. For a year she has told her husband, "I'd be happier if B.T. were not on the place.") She attempts to console Mattie until her loyal old servant exclaims, "Miss Harriet . . . it's like you losin' Mr. Son. B.T. is gwine too." At this comment Harriet reacts as if she had been slapped in the face:

> The small white woman abruptly withdrew her arms from about her servant. The movement was made in one fearful gesture which included the sudden contraction of her lips and the widening of her bright eyes. "Mattie!" she declaimed. "How dare you? That will be exactly enough from you!" . . . . Her face grew hot and cold alternately as her indignation rose and rose again. . . . She wondered first that she had refrained from striking Mattie out in the yard. . . . The open comparison of Son's departure to that sullen, stinking, thieving, fornicating black B.T. was an injury for which Son could not avenge himself, and she felt it her bounden duty to in some way make that black woman feel the grossness of her wrong and ultimately to drive her off the premises.

Although there is no further discussion of the devastating significance of this event, often troubling, unexpected developments do occur. She is appalled to hear her proper and gentlemanly son discussing with Ann Prewitt, the girl whom he has brought down from New York with him, the condition of her own health, that his mother went through menopause, as Son says, "years ago when I was still in school," obviously a subject no gentleman would discuss with a lady. Her perceptive and considerate son would not reveal a personal, intimate matter concerning his own mother to someone she hardly knows. The Buchanans, contrary to all established custom and accepted manners, entertain the Wilsons not in their own home but at the country club. (Because, Dr. Wilson says, their house is too small.) The two daughters cause considerable friction by baiting the girl Son has brought down from New York, an editor of a birth control magazine, and a woman of extremely liberal political persuasions, with conservative political opinions they have learned from the Nashville Agrarians. The climax really comes when Ann Prewitt reveals the true nature of her relationship with Son and something of what that seemingly exemplary young man is really like, some of his interests and attitudes which he has carefully concealed from his family. "He always thinks a person behaves badly," Ann says, "who doesn't amuse him. He cares nothing for anything I say except when I'm talking theory of some kind. He is very willing to bring me here before your friends to express all manner of opinion which they and you find disagreeable while he behaves with conventional good taste." Although he has been careful to maintain a perfectly innocent platonic relationship toward her, she has been so "vulgar as to fall in love with him." The weekend is not turning out at all as Harriet had expected it to.

As the reader learns what a cad and a hypocrite Son is—really not worthy to be compared to B.T.—Harriet hears Mattie's scream of grief. Suddenly, as if she has experienced a sudden jolt of illumination, Harriet realizes what a shambles her life actually is. Her family is really non-existent and even the pretense of family unity is rapidly nearing an end. None of her children has any intention of marrying. She has reduced all of them to mere abstractions, as she has Mattie and B.T., and the real emptiness of her life is revealed by her inability to comfort Mattie in her time of need because she is black and has the bad taste to compare her loss of B.T. to Harriet's loss of Son. Ironically, the unjustness of this comparison is not that B.T. does not merit comparison to Son but that Harriet is incapable of feeling the depth of genuine affection for anyone that Mattie has for the "drinking, stinking fornicating B.T." She goes to her room and lies on her bed, completely emptied of all strength, energy, and feeling:

> She thought of all the talking that Son and the girls had done and she felt that she was even beginning to understand what it had meant. But she sadly reflected that her children believed neither what Ann Prewitt nor what the professors at the University were offering them. To Harriet it seemed that her children no longer existed; it was as though they had all died in childhood as people's children used to do. All the while she kept remembering that Mattie was sitting out in that shack for the sole purpose of inhaling the odor in the stifling air of B.T.'s room.

These are the thoughts that pass through Harriet's mind when she realizes her inadequacies. She cannot assist another human being in her moment of greatest need because when she looks into Mattie's eyes, she sees not only grief and hostility but also "an unspeakable loneliness for which she could offer no consolation."

Allen Tate develops a disturbing picture of a society that has lost its traditions, as the one depicted in Peter Taylor's stories is in the process of doing. A social order without manners, religions, morals, or codes, Tate writes, always ends in chaotic or violent action. Taylor writes of social order in transition, as "A Long Fourth" and many of his other stories reveal, of a people moving from a closely knit, ordered community to an urbanized society, a people who are slowly losing their traditional values. Seldom does Taylor suggest that organized religion affects the behavior of his characters. Although there is the semblance of a social order composed of polite, well-mannered, civilized, compassionate people, there are too many loveless marriages, too much sham and hypocrisy, too many empty and meaningless gestures for us to put much faith in the stability of the materially acquisitive, thing-oriented society to which Taylor's characters belong. Too often a character is confronted by a crisis, as Harriet Wilson is, only to realize her aloneness, her essential loneliness, her conviction that she is the only human being ever to have been forced to face that specific problem. There is no one nor any established code of conduct with whom she can share her concern or consult for a possible solution.

Unlike Taylor's world of surface placidity, of mannerly, orderly behavior, and civilized social value, Cormac McCarthy's is one dominated by bestial passion and the primitive urge to survive. His technique is not that of the sensitive, perceptive artist recording the activities of people who seem to fashion their lives according to the rules of social decorum; instead McCarthy explores the innermost motives that drive men and women who do not possess, apparently, even the minimum amount of the qualities required for accepted moral behavior. Strangely enough, when the exterior covering is stripped away, one often finds that Taylor's characters and McCarthy's are very similar. The same compulsions move them despite their vastly different backgrounds and environments. Only the techniques of their creators differ. McCarthy is carrying forward the fictional technique often referred to as the Southern Gothic or the Grotesque, a manner of writing often associated with William Faulkner, Eudora Welty, Flannery O'Connor, and other important Southern writers. Artists of this persuasion are often accused of deliberate distortion, of incongruous combinations of the monstrous and unsavory created and employed for the sole reason of evoking a desired effect.

Cormac McCarthy was born in Providence, Rhode Island, in 1933, but he moved to Knox County, Tennessee, when he was three years old. After finishing high school in 1951, he enrolled in the University of Tennessee. His academic record there was unsatisfactory, and he was not allowed to re-enroll. Like William Faulkner and many other men of artistic talent before him, McCarthy apparently could not or would not make himself adapt to the restrictive environment of an academic community. He did well in the subjects he liked, or the ones he thought would aid him in the pursuit of a career in literature. The others, some of which were required for a degree from the University, he simply ignored. The next year, consequently, he spent wandering around the country doing odd jobs, thinking, reading, and, as he later expressed it, trying to "get my head straight." In 1953 he enlisted in the air force for four years. After his discharge he returned to the University, where he remained for three more years but left without taking a degree. He still could not force himself to do acceptable work in courses that did not appeal to his sense of need.

From earliest youth McCarthy had wanted to write and for many years he was almost completely engaged in an active but somewhat disorganized program of reading. His insatiable desire to read whatever he could find, plus the fact that during his second tenure at the University he spent an increasing amount of time writing, undoubtedly account, in large part, for his poor academic record. When he left the University, he had no fewer than three novels underway. In 1959 he singled out *The Orchard Keeper* and went to work on it in earnest, but the necessity of earning a living delayed its completion for several years. When it appeared in 1965, it was an immediate critical success, although it attracted few readers outside academic and professional circles, winning for its author the William Faulkner Foundation Award for the most outstanding first novel published in that year; *The Orchard Keeper* also won the Travel Award of the American Academy of Arts and Letters. During his travels in Europe on this award, McCarthy met and married Anne deLisle of Hamble, England.

After the appearance of his first novel, McCarthy received financial assistance from the Rockefeller Foundation and the Guggenheim Memorial Foundation; consequently he was able to devote his full time to writing. Since then, he has published three novels: *Outer Dark* (1968), *Child of God* (1975), and *Suttree* (1979), the last of which was begun before *The Orchard Keeper.*

Critical reaction to *The Orchard Keeper* was predictable. McCarthy, the critics insisted, inherited the tradition of Faulknerian grotesquerie. Although the prose "is lean," "packed with vivid imagery" and builds "its own force and intensity," its effectiveness is considerably inundated by "Faulknerian excesses" that tend to render the author's intentions almost inexplicable. What is obviously intended as a horror story ends as a sentimental novel that is more morose than tragic. "Cormac McCarthy's *The Orchard Keeper,* an impressive complex debut, was a recipient of the William Faulkner Award," one commentator writes, "contrary to rumor, the annual prize is *not* bestowed upon the first novels which best mimic the South's greatest master. But to its misfortune, *The Orchard Keeper* bore countless comparisons to Faulkner's novels. The story, chronicling young John Wesley's friendship with his father's murderer, echoes the major Faulkner themes: the criminal as hero, the interplay of language, memory and myth, and the overriding problem of survival." Among its many faults, most critics found it too derivative, and many readers could not tolerate such a concentrated dose of horror and violence, much of which seemed without aim or purpose. There is too much sin without redemption, too much horror that has no function but to furnish the reader a gratuitous emotional response. In this first novel McCarthy is always reminding his reader of how repulsive, inhumane, selfish, and hypocritical man is, but why he reiterates these well-known facts — in a seemingly endless series of episodes, each one of which is more horrible than the last — is difficult to determine.

In *Outer Dark,* however, McCarthy seems to have his material more firmly under control, the scenes of horror — incest, murder, and vampirism, among others — all combine to convince one, as no mere statement or statistical table can — of the depravity of human nature. A passage near the beginning of the novel sets the tone. Culla Holme is awakened from a dream:

> There was a prophet standing in the square with arms upheld in exhortation to the beggared multitude gathered there. A delegation of human ruin who attended him with blind eyes upturned and puckered stumps and leprous sores. The sun hung on the cusp of eclipse and the prophet spoke to them. This hour the sun would darken and all these souls would be cured of their afflictions before it appeared again. And the dreamer himself was caught up among the supplicants and when they had been blessed and the sun begun to blacken he did push forward and hold up his hand and call out. Me, he cried. Can I be cured? The prophet looked down as if surprised to see him there amidst such pariahs. The sun paused. He said: Yes, I think perhaps you will be cured. Then the sun buckled and dark fell like a shout.

The "dark" that fell comes from a shout. Holme's sister, with whom he has been sharing a bed, is trying to awaken him to tell him to go for the "granny-woman" because their baby is coming. He refuses to get "the old geechee nigger witch" because he is afraid she will tell; therefore the sister has to bear the child without assistance. After the child is born, Holme tells her it is dead and takes it into the woods and buries it alive. After his sister has recovered somewhat, she insists on seeing the child's

grave. After much begging and pleading from her, he takes her to the
spot where he has buried it. She scratches around in the ground looking
for the remains but can find nothing and concludes that her baby was
alive when her brother left it in the woods and that it has been taken
away by a tinker who visited their house just after the child was born.
(Both of her suppositions are correct, of course.) As soon as she is able,
she goes in search of her baby and her brother follows, looking for her.
The remainder of the novel is a bizarre kind of picaresque tale of their
wandering from one unimaginable horror to another. In their aimless
wanderings, Holme is falsely accused of causing two hundred hogs to
run over a cliff, an occurrence that results not only in their death but
also in that of one of the drovers. Holme escapes death from the
drover's friends, who intend to hang him, only by leaping from the cliff
as they are searching for a rope.

The tinker, whom a gang of misfits has captured and is forcing him to
accompany them on a series of raids on farms in the area, is hanged, and
his body is left in a tree for the vultures:

> The tinker in his burial tree was a wonder to the birds. The vultures
> that came by day to nose with their hooked beaks among his buttons
> and pockets like outrageous pets soon left him naked of his rags and
> flesh alike. Black mandrake sprang beneath the tree as it will where
> the seed of the hanged falls and in spring a new branch pierced his
> breast and flowered in a green boutonniere perennial beneath his yel-
> low grin. He took the sparse winter snows upon what thatch of hair
> still clung to his dried skull and hunters that passed that way never
> chanced to see him brooding among his barren limbs. Until wind had
> tolled the tinker's bones and seasons loosed them one by one to the
> ground below and alone his bleached and weathered brisket hung in
> that lonesome wood like a bone birdcage.

The three men who murder the tinker move mysteriously in and out of
the action of the narrative, explaining their motivation for committing
evil acts in a manner worthy of a character from a Flannery O'Connor
story. Their leader, a man named Harmon, explains to Culla Holme his
relationship to humankind: "You aint no different from the rest. From
any man borned and raised and have his own and die. They aint one
man in three got even a black suit to die in." At Harmon's command
Holme hands him the child produced by the incestuous union with his
sister: "It made no gesture at all. It dangled from his hands like a dressed
rabbit, a gross eldritch doll with ricketsprung legs and one eye opening
and closing softly like a naked owl's. He rose with it and circled the fire

and held it out toward the man. The man looked at it a moment and then took it with one hand by its upper arm and placed it between his feet." Then watching closely, Holme saw the second man of the trio draw a knife, the blade winking "in the light like a long cat's eye slant and malevolent and a dark smile erupted on the child's throat and went all broken down the front of it. The child made no sound." The third member of the group, a mute, "knelt forward. He was drooling and making little whimpering noises in his throat. . . . The man with the knife handed him the child, . . . [and] he seized it up, looked once at Holme with witless eyes and buried his moaning face in his throat."

The omnipresence of these three men, always appearing and disappearing in the most mysterious fashion, one critic believes, gives the novel the tone of a morality play: "The three men who ransack and murder are a brilliant device; a mad variation on the Magi, they skim about the perimeter of the tale and eventually bring the work to its justifiable conclusion."

The novel concludes with Holme's bidding farewell to a blind preacher, who may well be the prophet of the dream with which the novel opens. Holme says he must be "on his way." His "way" leads him down a strange road where for miles "there were only the charred shapes of trees in a dead land where nothing moved save windy rifts of ash that rose dolorous and died again down the blackened corridors." Late in the day he came to a swamp:

> Before him stretched a spectral waste out of which reared only the naked trees in attitudes of agony and dimly hominoid-like figures in a landscape of the damned. A faintly smoking garden of the dead that tended away to the earth's curve. He tried his foot in the mire before him and it rose in a vulvate welt claggy and sucking. He stepped back. A stale wind blew from this desolation and the marsh reeds and black ferns among which he stood clashed softly like things chained. He wondered why a road should come to such a place.

Many commentators have discussed McCarthy's uncanny ability to create precisely the kind of landscape to serve as setting for his strangely compelling stories, a land "with a disturbing quietude where actuality turns ever so gently into myth without sacrificing the necessary reality."

McCarthy is indeed a strange incompatible mixture, one that some critics believe is made of combining proper proportions of Greek dramatists and medieval moralists. Although we know that Lester Ballard destroys and is destroyed in *Child of God,* we do not know why, only that he is drawn by forces beyond his control. This novel is the clearest, most forceful statement to date of McCarthy's basic concerns. Early in the narrative Lester Ballard is described as "small, unclean, unshaven . . . with a constrained truculence. Saxon and Celtic bloods. A child of God much like yourself perhaps." If he is one day to be judged by God for the horrible crimes he commits, he may also, like many Greek heroes, be a pawn in the hands of the gods, driven by instincts, desires, and compulsions over which he has no control. He may act in the inexplicably horrible manner in which he does because control of his actions and his fate lies somewhere outside himself. Although we may not understand why Lester Ballard does the unbelievably terrible things he does—we simply cannot dismiss him as mad—there seems to be some order in the process of his self-destruction. We know little about his heritage, except that his grandfather did nothing in the Civil War "besides scout the bushes." Although he was not one of the many courageous men that Sevier County put into the Union army, he was one of the few who later drew a pension. About the only thing he did in that war that anyone remembers was that once when he deserted, some soldiers came to his house looking for him and while they were searching the barn and smokehouse, he slipped away, found the soldiers' horses, and cut enough leather from the sergeant's saddle to halfsole his shoes. We know, too, that Lester's father killed himself, when Lester was nine or ten, because his wife had run off with another man. The boy stood there without a word when they cut his father down from the barn rafter from which he had hanged himself. The boy's expression did not change when his father fell at his feet with his "eyes . . . run out on stems like a crawfish and his tongue blacker'n a chow dog's," but Lester never was the same after that experience. He incurred the ill will of his schoolmates when he became violent and cruelly punished a boy smaller than he who refused to act as Lester tried to make him. Lester grew up a "figure of wretched arrogance . . . [who] cursed or muttered or spat" after the cars that passed him on the road, an errant outsider who brutally assaulted community mores and the laws of decency and self-respect because of his feeling of not belonging, because he had neither the looks, the brains, the industry nor the family connections to gain the respect of the community. While he was still a boy, he "set fenceposts for eight cents a post" to get money to buy a rifle. He practiced until he was a crack shot, the best in the county, and demonstrated his skill by visiting a booth at the county fair and shooting small red dots from cardboard squares until he had won all the prizes the barker would allow. He won two "ponderous mohair" teddy bears and a tiger. He was a hero, envied by everyone there. From that time forward his rifle becomes an appendage of himself; he is never without it. It serves as a means of getting what he wants.

At every stage of his life he is forced to live more and more on a sub-human level. First his home is taken from him because he cannot pay the taxes. He moves into a hovel, and his only possessions are his rifle, the three stuffed animals he won at the fair, and a thin mattress. One night he burns that house down, trying to stay warm, and has to move into a cave. As his life becomes more elemental, more animalistic, he becomes more and more frustrated because his most primitive desires are not satisfied. He goes to see a dumpkeeper because he has some daughters Ballard is interested in: "The dumpkeeper had spawned nine daughters. . . . These gangling progeny with black hair hanging in their armpits now sat idle and wide-eyed day after day in chairs and crates about the little yard. . . . They moved like cats and like cats in heat attracted surrounding swains to their midden until the old man used to go out at night and fire a shotgun just to clear the air." Although these girls spread their favors with little discretion—one even included her father among her lovers—none of them will even look at Lester. Nearby is another family he calls on—the only other persons he sees socially—because in it there is an eligible daughter, one who has had an illegitimate child by a half-wit. Although Lester brings the child a present, a baby robin whose feet the child immediately gnaws off, the girl is not even civil to him.

Since he cannot have a legitimate affair, he becomes a voyeur, peeping into parked cars. Then he finds a girl who has been asphyxiated while making love. Since she can offer no resistance, he possesses her, "pouring into that waxen ear everything he'd ever thought of saying to a woman." He keeps her until she burns up in the house; then he moves by the half-mad logic that motivates him to the next stage: he takes his rifle and reduces the girls, including the one with the idiot child, to a stage in which he can control them. By this time he was living in the cave, and he placed the "bodies on stone ledges in attitudes of response" in a "tall bell-shaped cavern" with a cathedral-like ceiling: "Here the walls with their softlooking convolutions, slavered over as they were with wet and bloodred mud, had an organic look to them, like the innards of some great beast. Here in the bowels of the mountain Ballard turned his light on ledges or pallets of stone where dead people lay like saints." Lester Ballard is able to change the basic nature of depraved human flesh. Not only can he convert it to a form he can control, but he can erase its depravity. The dead bodies in the cave have returned to the innocence of the womb.

Intermittently, Lester has been watching the house that once belonged to him but is now occupied by another. Its present owner is a man named Greer who has acquired it by paying its delinquent taxes. In his maddened state Lester thinks if he disposes of Greer, the house will again be his. One day he tries to kill Greer, but his shot is accidentally deflected by a shovel. (Greer unexpectedly raises the shovel as Ballard squeezes the trigger.) He follows Greer into the house where he is met by a blast from Greer's shotgun. Although he does not die, he is taken from his hospital room by a group of vigilantes who insist they will kill him unless he shows them where he has hidden the bodies of the people he has killed. He escapes from this group only to die a few days later in his hospital room of pneumonia. After death he is subjected to a final act of dehumanization:

> There in a basement room he was preserved with formalin and wheeled forth to take his place with other deceased persons newly arrived. He was laid out on a slab and flayed, eviscerated, dissected. His head was sawed open and the brains removed. His muscles were stripped from his bones. His heart was taken out. His entrails were hauled forth and delineated and the four young students who bent over him like those haruspices of old perhaps saw monsters worse to come in their configurations. At the end of three months when the class was closed, Ballard was scraped from the table into a plastic bag and taken with others of his kind to a cemetery outside the city and there interred. A minister from the school read a simple service.

Child of God, as do McCarthy's other books, provides for the reader the quality of knowledge one can get only from art, and, despite the repulsive experiences that fill his novels, the truths of human nature that his unique narratives contain intrude upon the reader's consciousness in a compelling and unforgettable manner. McCarthy's style ranges from the philosophically ponderous, slow and heavy, to the pared-down, effectively straight-forward, disarmingly light; and his novels seem obsessed with disagreeable subjects—*Child of God* is filled with episodes of animalistic fornication, incest, murder, and necrophilia—but after reading any of his books the certainty of man's depravity no longer seems anything less than fundamental truth. Robert Coles, a professional psychiatrist who writes perceptively about modern literature, emphasizes the high seriousness of McCarthy's speculations: "Cormac McCarthy does not know why some men are haunted Ballards, while others live easily with kin and neighbors. He simply writes novels that tell us we cannot comprehend the riddles of human idiosyncrasy, the influence of the merely contingent or incidental upon our lives. He is a novelist of religious feeling who appears to subscribe to no creed but who cannot stop wondering in the most passionate and honest way what gives life meaning."

After reading McCarthy's novels, one is not likely ever again to underestimate the complexities of the world, nor is it easy to believe that he would reduce ultimate reality to a series of impressions and rules that he can circumscribe with his senses and his reason. Over man's activities, McCarthy's novels reiterate, there is always an apocalyptic cloud, one that will encourage his more perceptive readers to ponder the inexplicable mysteries of the world they must live in. Perhaps his greatest gift as a writer of fiction is to make us care about what happens to Lester Ballard and Culla Holme, despite the repulsion we feel because of the subhuman acts they commit. Now that Faulkner and Flannery O'Connor are dead, and the novels of Walker Percy, who some critics believe is the premier contemporary southern novelist, seem to be becoming more and more expository and rhetorical, serious readers of southern fiction have just cause to anticipate with eager impatience the publication of McCarthy's next book.

Limited space will permit only a cursory examination of the work of some of the other contemporary Tennesseans whose writing merits serious consideration. The first of these is Madison Jones, who was born in Nashville, Tennessee, on March 21, 1925. After receiving his B.A. degree from Vanderbilt, where he studied under Donald Davidson, he enrolled at the University of Florida, where he pursued his interest in fiction writing with Andrew Lytle. In addition to several short stories, which appeared in such literary journals as the *Sewanee Review,* Jones has published six novels: *The Innocent* (1957), *Forest of the Night* (1960), *A Buried Land* (1963), *An Exile* (1967) — made into a popular motion picture entitled "I Walk the Line" — *A Cry of Absence* (1971), and *Passage Through Gehenna* (1978).

Most of his fiction is set in Middle Tennessee and is concerned with man's attempt to live with dignity and purpose in a disintegrating society. Allen Tate has called Jones "one of the most important contemporary American writers," and Robert Penn Warren's opinion of Jones's literary talent is no less laudatory. "It would be no surprise to find, in the fullness of time," Warren has written, "this writer comfortably situated among the best of his generation." Many critics have observed Jones's narrative skill and his ability to integrate an idea into a narrative. To many, *A Cry of Absence* is among the few very good books written on the twentieth-century racial crisis in the South.

Although he was born in Nashville, Tennessee, on May 6, 1914, Randall Jarrell spent most of his boyhood in California and the Middle West. He returned to Nashville, however, to attend Hume-Fogg High School, from which he was graduated in 1931, and Vanderbilt University. At Vanderbilt he studied with Ransom and Davidson, and immediately after receiving his B.A. degree in 1935, Jarrell entered the graduate school there.

When Ransom left Vanderbilt in the autumn of 1937, Jarrell accompanied him and became instructor of English and tennis coach at Kenyon College. After receiving his M.A. degree in 1938, he moved from Kenyon to the University of Texas. Shortly after his marriage, on June 1, 1940, to Mackie Langham, his first collection of poems appeared, as a part of the volume *Five Young American Poets* (1941). The next year he published *Blood for a Stranger,* his first book of poems. In 1942 he joined the Eighth Air Force, and his war experiences motivated his best-known poem, "Death of the Ball Turrett Gunner."

At the end of the war, he returned to teaching—at Sarah Lawrence College, Princeton, and the University of North Carolina at Greensboro. His first marriage ended in divorce and in 1952 he married Mary Eloise van Shrader. Despite a full schedule of teaching he continued to write with increasing skill and dexterity. His *Little Friend, Little Friend* (1945) and *Losses* (1948), which brought his work to the attention of a broad circle of serious readers of poetry, was followed immediately by *The Seven League Crutches* (1951), and *Selected Poems* (1955). *Poetry and the Age* (1953) established his reputation as a critic with particularly keen perceptions of the basic problems confronting the modern artist. His only novel, *Pictures from an Institution* (1954) is one of the best examples of the corrective satiric narrative in American literature. Many critics believe some of his most impressive poetry is included in his last volume of verse, *The Woman at the Washington Zoo* (1960).

Jarrell was hospitalized in Chapel Hill, North Carolina, for a nervous breakdown; on October 14, 1965, he was killed when struck by an automobile in that city. His considerable contributions to American letters is obvious to the reader of the *Complete Poems* (1969).

Wilma Dykeman is another contemporary writer whose literary reputation should be higher. A biographer and social historian as well as a novelist, Dykeman was born in Asheville, North Carolina, but has lived for many years in Newport, Tennessee. Her three novels—*The Tall Woman* (1962), *The Far Family* (1966), and *Return the Innocent Earth* (1973)—all reflect her deep love of the Appalachian region. A theme running through them is the unique role of the mountain woman in her family and in the community. Like many other contemporary writers, Dykeman is concerned about the impact modern technology will have on traditional mountain society, especially how such endeavors as strip mining and modern methods of timber cutting are destroying the wilderness of the Appalachian mountains. Although a universal theme is embedded in all of her novels, her attention to Appalachian manners, customs, and beliefs is so acute and her ear for the rhythms of mountain speech so infallibly accurate that she is often dismissed merely as a regional writer. Her well-plotted, tightly structured, and carefully paced novels merit a wider critical audience.

Unlike Wilma Dykeman, Jesse Hill Ford, for a brief period, commanded the attention of both the popular audience and the literary community. His television drama, "The Conversion of Buster Drumwright." published as a book in 1964, was twice shown on national television, and the motion picture version of his novel, *The Liberation of Lord Byron Jones* (1965), was a popular success. His first novel, *Mountains of Gilead* (1961), and a collection of his early stories, *Fishes, Birds, and Sons of Men: Stories* (1967), were well received by reviewers and critics.

Born in Troy, Alabama, on December 28, 1928, Jesse Hill Ford grew up in Nashville, Tennessee, and attended Vanderbilt University (1947-51) and the University of Florida (1954-55). Like Madison Jones, he studied fiction writing with Davidson and Lytle and has publicly stated that they were the two persons who most influenced his writing. In addition to the work mentioned above, he has published *The Feast of Saint Barnabas* (1969), and *The Raider* (1975). All of his fiction, with the exception of *Saint Barnabas,* is set in West Tennessee. Much of it is filled with violence and hate, and his characters often find themselves so deeply involved in the complexities of a rapidly changing society that they are destroyed—emotionally and spiritually, if not physically. Of the work published to date, many critics argue that Ford's most significant literary achievements are to be found in his early stories, most of which are collected in *Fishes, Birds and Sons of Men.* In this volume are several excellent stories concerned with the process of maturation, the *rite de passage,* the passing from youth to manhood.

One contemporary Tennessee writer, David Madden, has been able to combine most successfully an academic and a literary career. Although he has taught full time since 1960, served as associate editor of *Fiction International* (since 1973), and as associate editor of the *Kenyon Review* (1964-66), he has written in that period nine books and edited nine others. A novelist, poet, playwright, and literary critic, Madden was born in Knoxville, Tennessee, and received his B.S. degree from the University of Tennessee in 1958. After earning the next year his M.A. from San Francisco State, he attended the Yale Drama School in 1960. He has taught at Centre College, University of Louisville, Kenyon College, Ohio University, and Louisiana State University.

His work in the several literary genres in which he has been engaged has been well received, but his greatest skill seems to be in the short story, for which he has won several awards, including a commendation from the National Council on the Arts. Two of his stories, "The Day the Flowers Came" (1969) and "No Trace" (1971), were included in *Best American Short Stories* in the years the stories were published. In spite of his prolific output, Madden is a careful craftsman, and his work is characterized by a breadth of imaginative power that only the best of creative writers possess.

Two other academicians have not been able to integrate as well as Madden the different demands of a writing and a teaching career. Born in East Tennessee in 1933, Richard Marius was graduated from the University of Tennessee and afterwards received a Ph.D. degree in history from Yale University. As a professional historian, Marius taught first at Gettysburg College and subsequently for fourteen years (1964–78) at the University of Tennessee, Knoxville. He moved in 1978 to the faculty of Harvard, where he became director of that university's expository writing program. His full-time teaching career, as well as his historical publications—such as *Luther,* co-editing Thomas More's *Confutation,* and extensive contributions to scholarly journals—have left limited time for Marius to pursue a concurrent career as a novelist. Nonetheless, he has produced two novels, *The Coming of Rain* (1969) and *Bound for the Promised Land* (1976). The former has a post-Civil War East Tennessee setting and focuses in part upon the religion of the region. The reception these two books have received should encourage him to write others. Marius's motivation for writing seems to be close to that which prompted William Faulkner to mine his "little postage stamp of earth." Marius once said that he writes because "I am going to die and I don't want to perish completely from the earth."

The career of Walter Sullivan is not far different from that of Marius. Because of demanding academic commitments—including publishing more than a hundred critical essays and two books of literary criticism, *Death by Melancholy* (1972) and *A Requiem for the Renascence* (1976) —he has published a handful of short stories and only two novels, *Sojourn of a Stranger* (1957) and *The Long, Long Love* (1959). Since 1949 he has taught contemporary literature at Vanderbilt, where he received his undergraduate degree. He also earned an MFA degree from the State University of Iowa. Sullivan's critical writing has earned him the reputation of being one of the most influential and provocative commentators on modern writers, whose point of view, unlike that of most of his contemporaries, is always that of the traditional Christian.

Now considered one of the most significant of the young black poets, Yolande Cornelia Giovanni ("Nikki") was born on June 7, 1943, in Knoxville, but as a young child she moved with her family to Cincinnati, Ohio. She returned to Knoxville, however, to attend high school. In 1967 she was graduated from Fisk University with a major in history. In college she became an avid political activist, an interest she continued during her graduate work at Pennsylvania and Columbia. She withdrew from both schools without taking a degree and immediately began to devote almost all of her time and energy to the problems confronting black Americans, appearing on many television talk shows and lecturing before college audiences across America. She is now a member of the faculty of Livingston College of Rutgers University. Giovanni's work includes *Black Feeling, Black Talk* (1968), *Black Judgment* (1969), *Re: Creation* (1970). Her intense interest in the plight of the American black is well represented in *James Baldwin and Nikki Giovanni: A Dialogue* and *A Poetic Equation: Conversation Between Nikki Giovanni and Margaret Walker* (1974).

Although many critics believe the southern renascence ended about 1950, there seems to have been no noticeable decrease in the number of books of unquestioned literary quality written within the past thirty years by Tennessee authors. The four contemporary writers whose work we have examined in some detail, as well as many of those who have received an often undeservedly briefer treatment, have made serious and successful attempts to reconstitute the essentials of human experience. In their writings, too, they have employed many of the remarkable advances in literary technique that have been developed by the writers of the Western World in this century.

Selected Checklist of Books

PRIMARY SOURCES

Under primary sources are the most significant books of Tennessee writers that I was unable to mention or discuss in the text, for the most part.

AGEE, JAMES

The best of Agee's reviews are included in *Agee on Film: Reviews and Comments*; major movie scripts are reproduced in *Agee on Film: Five Film Scripts*; the most intimate revelations of his private and artistic concerns are in the *Letters of James Agee to Father Flye*.

BROOKS, CLEANTH

Brooks also was co-editor of several other influential textbooks: *An Approach to Literature,* with R.P. Warren and J.T. Purser (1936, 1939, 1952, 1964, 1975); *Understanding Fiction,* with R.P. Warren (1943, 1959); *Understanding Drama,* with R.B. Heilman (1949); *Modern Rhetoric,* with R.P. Warren (1949, 1958, 1972); and *American Literature: the Makers and the Making,* with R.P. Warren and R.W.B. Lewis (1973). His important critical books include — in addition to *Modern Poetry and the Tradition* (1939) — *The Well Wrought Urn: Studies in the Structure of Poetry* (1947); *Literary Criticism, A Short History,* with W.K. Wimsatt (1957); *The Hidden God: Studies in Hemingway, Faulkner, Yeats, Eliot and Warren* (1963); *William Faulkner: the Yoknapatawpha Country* (1963); *American Literature: A Mirror, Lens or Prism?* (1967); *A Shaping Joy: Studies in the Writer's Craft* (1971); *William Faulkner: Toward Yoknapatawpha and Beyond* (1978).

DAVIDSON, DONALD

Davidson published another textbook, *British Poetry of the Eighteen-Nineties* (1937); a collection of poetry, *Lee in the Mountains and Other Poems Including The Tall Men* (1949); and an impressive two-volume history of the Tennessee River, *The Tennessee* (1946, 1948), in the Rivers of America series. A collection of his essays, *Still Rebels, Still Yankees and Other Essays,* appeared in 1957; *The Southern Writer in the Modern World* (Eugenia Blount Lamar Memorial Lectures) in 1958, and a new collection of poems, *The Long Street* in 1961. In 1963 John Tyree Fain published a selection of the reviews Davidson had contributed to *The Tennessean, The Spyglass: Views and Reviews,* and in 1966 the collected poems, *Poems 1922-1961,* were issued.

TATE, ALLEN

Tate's industrious career continued almost unabated until the year of his death. Some of his best-known critical essays, including "Tension in Poetry," "Literature as Knowledge," and "What is a Traditional Society?" appeared in *Reason in Madness: Critical Essays* (1941). "Seasons of the Soul," which some critics consider Tate's most enduring poem, was included in *Poems: 1925-1947* (1948). The *Essays of Four Decades* (1970), *Memoirs and Opinions* (1976), and the *Collected Poems 1919-1976* (1977) were his last published volumes.

TAYLOR, PETER

The best of Taylor's writing is included in the following: *A Woman of Means* (1950), *The Widows of Thornton* (1954), *Tennessee Day in Saint Louis: A Comedy* (1957), *Happy Families are all Alike: A Collection of Stories* (1959), *Miss Leonora When Last Seen and Fifteen Other Stories* (1963), *A Stand in the Mountains* (1965), *The Collected Stories* (1969), *Presences* (1973), *As Darker Grows the Night* (1976), *In the Miro District and Other Stories* (1977).

WARREN, ROBERT PENN

Warren's twelve books of fiction are *Night Rider* (1939), *At Heaven's Gate* (1943), *All the King's Men* (1946), *World Enough and Time* (1950), *Band of Angels* (1955), *The Cave* (1959), *Wilderness* (1961), *Flood* (1964), *Meet Me in the Green Glen* (1971), and *A Place to Come to* (1977), *Blackberry Winter* (short stories, 1946), and *The Circus in the Attic* (short stories, 1948). His twelve books of poetry are *Thirty-six Poems* (1935), *Eleven Poems on the Same Theme* (1942), *Selected Poems, 1923-1943* (1944), *Brother to Dragons* (1953), *Promises: Poems 1954-56* (1957), *You, Emperors, and Other Poems, 1957-1960* (1960), *Selected Poems New and Old, 1923-1966* (1966), *Incarnations: Poems 1966-1968* (1968), *Audubon: A Vision* (1969), *Or Else: Poems 1968-1974* (1974), *Selected Poems, 1923-1975* (1977), and *Brother to Dragons: A New Version* (1979), *Being Here* (   ). He is the author of a drama,

All the King's Men: A Play (1960), a collection of critical essays, *Selected Essays* (1958), and five books of social, political, and cultural criticism: *Segregation, The Inner Conflict in the South* (1956), *The Legacy of the Civil War* (1961), *Who Speaks for the Negro?* (1956), *A Plea in Mitigation: Modern Poetry and the End of an Era* (1966) and *Democracy and Poetry* (1975). His most important textbooks are mentioned in the text; his others include: *Six Centuries of Great Poetry* (with Albert Ershine, 1955), *A New Southern Harvest: An Anthology* (with Erskine, 1954), *The Scope of Fiction* (with Cleanth Brooks, 1960), *Faulkner: A Collection of Critical Essays* (1966). This list, of course, does not include all of Warren's publications.

SECONDARY SOURCES

Included in this checklist are secondary sources that might be of special interest to persons who want to learn more about Tennessee writers.

Barson, Alfred T. *A Way of Seeing: A Critical Study of James Agee.* Boston: Univ. of Massachusetts Press, 1972.

Bishop, Ferman. *Allen Tate.* New York: Twayne, 1967.

Bohner, Charles H. *Robert Penn Warren.* New York: Twayne, 1964.

Bradbury, John M. *The Fugitives: A Critical Account.* Chapel Hill: Univ. of North Carolina Press, 1958.

Buffington, Robert. *The Equilibrist: A Study of John Crowe Ransom's Poems, 1916–1963.* Nashville: Vanderbilt Univ. Press, 1967.

Cary, Richard. *Mary W. Murfree.* New York: Twayne, 1967.

Cowan, Louise. *The Fugitive Group: A Literary History.* Baton Rouge: Louisiana State Univ. Press, 1959.

Fain, J.T., and T.D. Young, eds., *The Literary Correspondence of Donald Davidson and Allen Tate.* Athens: Univ. of Georgia Press, 1974.

Griffith, Albert J. *Peter Taylor.* New York, Twayne, 1970.

Guttenberg, Barnett. *Web of Being: The Novels of Robert Penn Warren.* Nashville: Vanderbilt Univ. Press, 1975.

Hemphill, George. *Allen Tate* (American Writers Pamphlet, 39). Minneapolis: Univ. of Minnesota Press, 1964.

Hubbell, Jay B. *The South in American Literature: 1607–1900.* Durham: Duke Univ. Press, 1954.

Karanikas, Alexander. *Tillers of a Myth.* Madison: Univ. of Wisconsin Press, 1966.

Kramer, Victor. *James Agee.* New York: Twayne, 1975.

Larsen, Erling. *James Agee* (American Writers Pamphlet, 95). Minneapolis: Univ. of Minnesota Press, 1971.

Longley, John Lewis, ed. *Robert Penn Warren: A Collection of Critical Essays.* New York: New York Univ. Press, 1954.

_____. *Robert Penn Warren* (Southern Writers Series, No 2). Austin: Steck-Vaughn, 1969.

Madden, David, ed. *Remembering James Agee.* Baton Rouge: Louisiana State Univ. Press, 1974.

Matthiessen, F.O. *American Renaissance.* New York: Oxford Univ. Press, 1941. See pp. 641–45.

McDowell, Frederick P.W. *Caroline Gordon* (American Writers Pamphlet, 59). Minneapolis: Univ. of Minnesota Press, 1966.

Meiners, R.K. *The Last Alternative: A Study in the Works of Allen Tate.* Denver: Alan Swallow, 1962.

Moreau, Genevieve. *The Restless Journey of James Agee.* New York: Morrow, 1977.

Ohlin, Peter H. *Agee.* New York: Obolensky, 1966.

Parks, Edd Winfield. *Charles Egbert Craddock.* Chapel Hill: Univ. of North Carolina Press, 1941.

Parsons, Thornton H. *John Crowe Ransom.* New York: Twayne, 1969.

Pells, Richard. *Radical Visions and American Dreams.* New York: Harper, 1973.

Purdy, Rob Roy, ed. *Fugitives Reunion: Conversations at Vanderbilt, May 3–5, 1956.* Nashville: Vanderbilt Univ. Press, 1959.

Rickels, Milton. *George Washington Harris.* New York: Twayne, 1965.

Riley, Carolyn, ed. *Contemporary Literary Criticism.* Detroit: Gale Research, 1975. See "Cormac McCarthy," pp. 341–44.

Rock, Virginia J. "The Making and Meaning of *I'll Take My Stand*: A Study in Utopian Conservatism," 1925–1939. Unpubl. diss., Univ. of Minnesota, 1961.

Rubin, Louis D., Jr. *The Wary Fugitives: Four Poets and the South.* Baton Rouge: Louisiana State Univ. Press, 1978.

_____. *The Faraway Country.* Seattle: Univ. of Washington Press, 1963.

_____, and Robert Jacobs, ed. *The Southern Renascence.* Baltimore: Johns Hopkins Univ. Press, 1953.

Seib, Kenneth. *James Agee: Promise and Fulfillment.* Pittsburgh: Univ. of Pittsburgh Press, 1968.

Squires, Radcliffe. *Allen Tate: A Literary Biography.* New York: Pegasus, 1971.

_____, ed. *Allen Tate and His Work: Critical Evaluations.* Minneapolis: Univ. of Minnesota Press, 1972.

Simpson, Lewis P. *The Dispossessed Garden.* Athens: Univ. of Georgia Press, 1975.

_____, ed. *The Possibilities of Order: Cleanth Brooks and His Work.* Baton Rouge: Louisiana State Univ. Press, 1977.

Strandberg, Victor H. *The Poetic Vision of Robert Penn Warren.* Lexington: Univ. Press of Kentucky, 1977.

Stuckey, W.J. *Caroline Gordon.* New York: Twayne, 1972.

Sullivan, Walter. *A Requiem for the Renascence.* Athens: Univ. of Georgia Press, 1976.

Watkins, Floyd C. *The Death of Art: Black and White in the Recent Southern Novel.* Athens: Univ. of Georgia Press, 1970.

West, Paul. *Robert Penn Warren* (American Writers Pamphlet, 44). Minneapolis: Univ. of Minnesota Press, 1964.

Williams, Miller. *The Poetry of John Crowe Ransom.* New Brunswick: Rutgers Univ. Press, 1972.

Wilson, Edmund. *Patriotic Gore.* New York: Oxford Univ. Press, 1966. See pp. 508–18.

Young, T.D., and M.T. Inge. *Donald Davidson.* New York: Twayne, 1971.

Young, T.D. *Gentleman in a Dustcoat: A Biography of John Crowe Ransom.* Baton Rouge: Louisiana State Univ. Press, 1976.

_____, ed. *John Crowe Ransom: Critical Essays and A Bibliography.* Baton Rouge: Louisiana State Univ. Press, 1968.

_____. *John Crowe Ransom* (Southern Writers Series, No. 12). Austin: Steck-Vaughn, 1971.

_____, ed. *The New Criticism and After.* Charlottesville: Univ. Press of Virginia, 1976.

Index

Other Tennessee Three Star Books

Visions of Utopia
Nashoba, Rugby, Ruskin, and the "New Communities"
    in Tennessee's Past
by John Egerton

Our Restless Earth
The Geologic Regions of Tennessee
by Edward T. Luther

Tennessee Strings
The Story of Country Music in Tennessee
by Charles K. Wolfe

Paths of the Past
Tennessee, 1770–1970
by Paul H. Bergeron

Civil War Tennessee
Battles and Leaders
by Thomas L. Connelly

Tennessee's Indian Peoples
From White Contact to Removal, 1540–1840
by Ronald N. Satz

Religion in Tennessee, 1777–1945
by Herman A. Norton

Tennessee's Three Presidents
by Frank B. Williams, Jr.

Blacks in Tennessee, 1791–1970
by Lester C. Lamon

Tennessee Writers
by Thomas Daniel Young

THE UNIVERSITY OF TENNESSEE PRESS : KNOXVILLE